The Last Cast

Pro-actively fishing with grace

by
WILLIAM H. COX

Unless otherwise indicated, all scripture was taken from the King James Version of the Bible.

ISBN-13: 978-0692095577 (Rusty Iron Ranch, LLC)

ISBN-10: 0692095578

Other books written by William H. Cox

Skies Are Not Cloudy All Day – *Is God trying to get your attention?*

The unconditional love of
A Dog's Love

Books available on Amazon & through website below:
www.rustyironranchllc.com

Mail:
Rusty Iron Ranch, LLC.
P.O. Box 1582
Sandpoint, Idaho 83864
e-mail: *jumpcreek113@yahoo.com*

THE LAST CAST

Pro-actively fishing with grace

Dedicated to Dad and his love for fishing.

Lloyd M. Cox

"Now unto him that is able to do exceeding abundantly above all that we ask or think, according to the power that worketh in us, Unto him be glory in the church by Christ Jesus throughout all ages, world without end. Amen"

Ephesians 3:20-21

Preface

My lineage stems from a long line of fishermen. Dad's side of the family homesteaded north of Belgrade, Montana over five generations ago out on Dry Creek. Every other year since I can remember, Dad, my uncle Larry, and I would go to visit my uncle Wallace on the ranch. We would spend a week fishing the East Fork of the Gallatin, Spring Creek and the Missouri River for those elusive brown trout.

In 1979 I moved to Montana and attended school at Montana State University. That was where I met Dan Danielson one of the finest fishermen I have ever known. Not so much because he is a good fisherman as much as for his love of fishing and his great sense of humor. Meeting him had a detrimental impact on my first year of college. Most students party their first year of school, my demise was fishing.

I was fortunate to have followed in step with a family that lived for fishing. When I was attending MSU, I remember going out to the ranches along the East Fork of the Gallatin River and introducing myself to the landowners. When they asked if I was related to Bud, Wallace or Larry Cox, they immediately said, "yes" welcoming me with a smile to fish anywhere I wanted on the place. It revealed to me the character of my family and their love for fishing.

Over the years I have had the pleasure of fishing with a wide variety of people. Each fishing trip has been an experience in itself with the most memorable ones leaving me laughing so hard I couldn't cast. Many of those trips, the sweet memories I stashed in my creel outnumbered the fish I caught.

When we first start out fishing we are uncoordinated, more or less a hazard to anyone within casting distance. Those brave souls that introduce us to fishing grace us with a limited amount of patience. With dedication, determination, and tenacity, fishing eventually becomes safer and even enjoyable for us and those around us.

Eventually, we learn through the many snags and backlashes we endure along the way, that these struggles help to refine our technique into a fine art that ultimately defines us.

Some of us are highly competitive; these fishermen characterize themselves in their ability to be successful. Purists have a multitude of rules and regulations on just how to fish legalistically. While still others are passive and take whatever swims their way. For them, fishing is just an excuse to get out in the mountains. Then there are those who fish by grace using anything they can to get one in the boat. They all have one thing in common. If you were to ask any of them, they would say that fishing is what brings them closest to God. It isn't so much the catching of fish that brings us closer as it is being out in that pristine environment that touches us so deeply. I was thinking about God and His desire to have a relationship with us, when I came to a realization.

When God created us, He gave each of us a very precious gift. That gift is the choice to love one another by *free will*. It is actually a double edged sword. We can choose to love anyone we choose or to hold back love just as well. Likewise, we can either accept someone's love or reject it. By free will it is completely up to us.

If you think about it, it is like a superpower, and God has given it to us to use for good or evil. The funny thing is, that a majority of people go through life never realizing the potential they leave the house with every day. This love through *free will* is the greatest gift that we could ever give someone. Whether it is from a husband to a wife, a mother to a son, a daughter to a dad, to people at work, school, or even people we pass by on the street. The *free will* choice of love can change the direction, good or bad, to anyone's day and can even have a substantial impact on a person's entire life. It has the potential to change a person's path in life just as well.

God loves us so much that He gave us that free gift of love, through His Son, Jesus. Jesus died for us as a perfect sacrifice for our sins, it is by our acceptance of that gift Jesus freely gave us which we are saved by with His grace through faith. That particular *free will* choice has eternal consequences.

Ephesians 2:8-9 *For by grace are ye saved through faith; and that not of yourselves:* it is *the gift of God: Not of works, lest any man should boast.*

God gave us that choice also as an example for us to pass along to those we run into along the trail.

Jesus said in John 13:34-35 *"A new commandment I give unto you, That ye love one another; as I have loved you, that ye also love one another. By this shall all men know that ye are My disciples, if ye have love one to another."*

Through the universal language of fishing and humor, I hope to share some of my learning experiences that God has blessed me with through fishing. I hope you identify with these short stories from when I first began to take up fishing in the irrigation ditch out back to the backcountry of Idaho and Montana. Through this cycle of life, it is my hope that this book brings you laughter and more importantly a realization of the deep, awesome love that Jesus has for each of us.

William H. Cox

A Countdown to the Beginning

"Four hundred ninety-eight, four hundred ninety-nine, five hundred! Okay, it's my turn!"

Monica didn't flinch "Hold on, he's almost in the bucket!" she whispered back impatiently.

"You said that five minutes ago! It's my turn." I demanded.

My younger sister ignored me.

Frustration was building up inside of me. It wasn't fair. I was the one who found this big minnow's lair, and I was the one who came up with the idea of using a bucket to catch it in the small concrete headgate.

This minnow was much smarter than all of the smaller ones combined. They would swim into the bucket without a care in the world but this big shiner would hang in the current just outside the bucket opening and venture no further. Monica and I had taken turns trying to catch him all week. As soon as I got off the bus I raced home, changed into my favorite green Levis and lucky high-top sneakers with the hole in the toe, and headed out to the ditch to catch that minnow. He was so big that he almost fulfilled the length requirements for an actual fish! This shiner had us completely hooked on our pursuit to catch him.

As soon as I got off the bus Monica was at my side. She was a year younger than me and went everywhere I did. Mom constantly lectured me every time we went outside," Watch out for your sister."

She needed watching out for, that's for sure! Being a year younger, she was constantly trying to outdo me in everything. I didn't care if she succeeded or not. It usually didn't work out all that well for her anyway. Like the time, we were climbing a tree; she wanted to out-climb me and ended up falling out and breaking her arm! Nothing ever slowed her down. Monica was competitive in everything. Right now, I just wanted to catch that fish. It wasn't about competition; it was a deep primal urge welling up inside of me that I was struggling to understand myself. It was fishing!

Due to my younger sister's continuous complaints, Mom insisted that I share the bucket time with her. It just wasn't fair. If mom knew how much she hogged the bucket, she would tell Monica to share and not me. I thought about telling Dad but he would not tolerate the squabbling and then neither one of us would be able to fish anymore.

The more I saw Monica's butt up in the air leaning over the headgate, the more it irritated me. I knew any

second my mom was going to call us in to dinner, and I
would not get another chance to fish until after school
the following day. "Man, this is so unfair", I thought.

"C'mon Monica, it's my turn!" I pleaded.

Again, she ignored me so I reached out and pushed her
butt. She dropped the bucket and caught herself but
not before she got a good dousing in the dirty irrigation
water. She came up out of the ditch boiling mad. Her
blonde braided pigtails dripping with water, screaming
at the top of her lungs, she headed straight for the
house. I yelled at her to stop or we were both going to
get in trouble but she never heard a word over her
incessant screaming, "Mom! Bill pushed me in the
ditch!"

I desperately grabbed the floating bucket and stuck it
down in the cool water. I knew the fury that was soon
to be coming from the house, and figured I better get as
much fishing in while I could. I heard Monica slam the
door to the house and had one ear strained to listen for
the rebuke while also trying to focus on the large shiner.
In a daring attempt, the large minnow took advantage
of my inability to multi-task and suddenly darted all the
way in the bucket and came back out taunting me. I was
so concerned about the onslaught to be unleashed from
the house that I hadn't been concentrating. *"Focus Bill,
you could have had him right there!"* I thought. The
minnow turned facing the bucket opening while
treading water, the way fish do with that cocky smile.

"C'mon please go in the bucket." I pleaded.

Then the words came thundering from the house "WILLIAM HENRY! Get in here NOW!"

Those words immediately turned my stomach sour as the wrath of Mom kicked in.

Running towards the house, weakness gradually seeped into my arms and legs. It was like an out of body experience in slow motion. Opening the screen door and walking into the house I attempted to muster up the most innocent face possible. "Yes? What's going on?"

"Did you push your sister into the ditch?" The intensity on my mom's face was that of an irrationally overwhelmed, crazy woman with one too many children on her plate. I just happened to be the child that pushed her over that invisible line, again. It was my intent to keep her just inside of "unhinged" but it was a fine line. Obviously, my strategy needed some work.

"Well, yes, kind of... by accident." I stammered "See, it was my turn with the bucket and see, well, she wouldn't share the bucket." I explained. Mother looked at Monica with a disapproving eye and I took advantage of it.

"Honestly, I didn't think that I pushed her hard enough to make her fall in. She's kind of a klutz. I mean, I barely even nudged her!" I continued.

"No sir!" Monica exploded "He shoved me in all the way on purpose!"

I looked up at my mom with innocence in my eyes, pleading with all of my heart.

"Both of you go to your room! Now!" Mom demanded, "Your father will be home any minute!"

Monica and I both looked at each other with wide eyes. We both knew what that meant. We were going to get a spanking.

I sat on my bed completely distraught. What kind of story could I come up with? I had taken note how using the "not sharing" had turned the tide ever so slightly in my favor with mom. But would it work with Dad? He was no-nonsense. Period.

Suddenly I heard Dad's truck pull up in the driveway. My hands were sweating, fear coursed through my veins as I heard the kitchen door open. I strained to hear what was being said but all I got was whispered mumbling from mom. "Your son, something, something, something..."

Dad's heavy steps came down the hall. My heart stopped when he paused at the door. I let out a breath that seemed like I had been holding for five minutes when I heard Monica's bedroom door open. I could hear her playing the crying card.

"Man, Dad will probably fall for that," I thought. My mind raced for what I was going to say and then sheer panic set in. My mind went blank. I forgot everything I had planned to say.

Suddenly the door burst wide open. Dad filled the doorway, and he was not happy. "What do you have to say for yourself young man?" he demanded.

Nothing. I had nothing. Couldn't come up with a thing. I just stood there fumbling with my hands.

"Sometimes I wonder about you! What were you thinking? She could have drowned," He continued. "I am going to go get the paddle. Both of you are getting a spanking, and you are grounded from fishing for a week."

"But Dad... ," I said in complete horror.

Dad turned back. His glare erased anything I had planned to say.

"Yes sir," I said respectfully.

When the door closed, thoughts flew rampant through my mind. "No fishing? That was a little much!" The stern look in his eyes came back to me. Then it hit me. *Oh man! This was going to get painful real soon!*

I have to say that God blessed me with a creative mind for solving problems at an early age and it suddenly occurred to me that I needed padding, a lot, of padding.

In seconds I had my favorite green Levis off and was pulling on an additional set of underwear when I heard Monica get the first swat. She let out a howl that shook the house. I had to hurry! I frantically got the third pair of underwear on but didn't quite get my pants back on, and buttoned when dad walked in with the paddle. I dropped my hands to my side as quickly as possible but my timing was off just enough to get busted. It didn't help having all the extra underwear bunched up at the top of my pants and my shirt was not tucked in on one side. Not to mention that the top drawer to my dresser was wide open and almost empty.

"Are you putting on extra underwear?" Dad said with surprise. The way he said it, was like a challenge.

I was busted so badly, I didn't even bother to respond. That was one of those rhetorical questions anyway. Trying to answer one of those had got me in trouble before.

"Drop your pants and grab your ankles." He demanded.

"Oh this was going to hurt!" I did as he said and the board responded with a "Swack!" on my bare butt. I got two more before I howled much louder than Monica!

"You stay in your room until dinner. I want you to think about what you have done." Dad said, before closing the door firmly.

I put my pants back on. *"Boy, that sure didn't work as planned,"* I thought. I wiped the excess tears from my eyes and lay back on my bed staring at the ceiling. A gentle breeze blew the curtain window open and fresh country air flowed in from outside. *"No fishing for a week, man... It might as well be for the entire summer!"* All I could think about was that fish swimming to the back of the bucket and out, relentlessly taunting me in my mind.

The next day was Friday; school seemed to drag on forever. Normally I would have been excited about the coming weekend. I would have been planning my strategy to be out in the ditch all weekend catching frogs and water snakes. I was sure that I would have devised a plan to have caught that fish too. Now, I was completely banned from the ditch. Now, there was nothing to do. My buddy, Jim looked at me with pity. "Sorry about your luck Bill." He patted my shoulder as he rose to get off at his bus stop.

I sulked on the long bus ride home staring out the window at the passing countryside. As the bus passed a pond nestled in between a couple of fields of dairy cows, I got a brilliant idea.

Everyone slept in on Saturday morning. If I got up at the crack of dawn, I could fish for an hour and sneak back into bed. They would never know! *"This was brilliant!"* I thought. The rest of the bus trip home I formulated my plan. It had to be well thought out and

20

foolproof. When I got off the bus I was the epitome of the perfect child. I was nice to all four of my sisters and helped set the table for dinner. I even helped do the dishes. When it was time for bed mom never had to tell me twice. I lay in bed staring up at the ceiling imagining that large minnow swimming into that red bucket.

The next morning I woke up right on cue. It was barely light out. Quietly I got out of bed and put on my green Levis and lucky high-top sneakers with the hole in the toe. I snickered to myself when I took an extra blanket and tucked it in under the covers. I had seen this trick on *Gunsmoke*, it was ingenious! No one would ever know!

Ever so silently I went up the stairs and out the front of the house. I was quite proud of how expertly I opened and shut the door without as much as a click. *"I should be an undercover spy,"* I complimented myself.

The sun was barely cresting over the horizon shooting beams of warm, yellow light across the landscape. I took a deep breath filling my lungs with refreshing, cool morning air as I walked quietly across the gravel driveway towards the irrigation ditch. Not even the neighbors were awake. What a glorious day to be alive! A mourning dove called its love song to another suitor and in the distance two mallard drakes pursued a hen weaving low across the recently planted cornfield in back, quacking dramatically. I avoided the headgate where the original offense occurred opting for the other side of the road. A leopard frog jumped into the ditch as I got near. The concentric rings from the splash floated away in the current.

Plunging the bucket into the cool water brought an exhilarating sense of excitement and built up anticipation. *"This is what it's all about,"* I surmised.

I held the red bucket as still as I could against the current. Smaller minnows tested the bucket in their curiosity. I quietly hoped that they would act as live decoys, providing a false sense of security for the large minnow. I remained absolutely still.

Eventually, the cold water worked its way into my arm causing my fingers to go numb. Over and over in my mind, I practiced pulling the bucket up at breakneck speed with the large minnow inside. Glancing around I could tell it was getting close to the time to head back to the house. Suddenly out of the corner of my eye I saw all of the smaller fish exit the bucket, dashing for the safety of the shadows. With a swish of its thick tail, the monster of all minnows appeared from the depths of the culvert and I froze. He was probably five inches long. *"Oh, I want this fish."*

It might have been the whites of my widened eyes that spooked him or maybe he read my mind through some sort of primeval game-prey telepathy, but in a flash, he was gone. Ever so slowly I leaned over, peering down into the water and saw him back in the dark shadows of the culvert. He was impressive sitting there with his gills vacillating back and forth. Ever so slowly I pulled my face back from the water's surface in hopes he would go in the bucket. The further I backed off, the more the reflection of the morning sky danced on the water's surface, impairing my view into the bucket. I got caught in my reflection dancing on the surface of the water when to my horror; an image appeared in the reflection causing me to gasp. It was a giant hand which came into view just over my right shoulder. I dropped the bucket and wheeled around to see Dad towering over me with a stern look on his face!

"What are you doing young man?" He said in an unnervingly calm voice.

I turned and stood up facing him stuttering, "Dad, I am sorry. It's.... just... this fish... well... it is so big!" My eyes welled up with tears. Dad's stern face softened up a bit which wasn't very much for him. "Grab that bucket and get back to the house."

I hurried to retrieve the bucket floating down the ditch. I knew I was on borrowed time now. *"Oh man, this was a doozy!"*

Heading back to the house, I noticed dad's hair was uncombed; he was wearing his white undershirt and jeans. His belt wasn't buckled and he didn't have any shoes or socks on.

"That's why I couldn't hear him," I theorized. I had to wonder though, how was he so quiet sneaking up on me because he sure had a hard time walking back across the gravel road and up the driveway barefoot?

I walked next to him back to the house, silently, staring at the ground. "You know I have to give you a spanking don't you?" He said almost apologetically.

"Yeah, I know," I said.

Dad waited most of the day before he came to give me that spanking. The waiting was actually worse than the spanking itself. I just wanted the punishment to be done with so I could relax. I was thinking I might have gotten away with it when he caught up with me around 4:30 that afternoon. My heart sank, and I stood in front of him looking at the ground. I sure wasn't going to try to put on another pair of underwear that's for sure. My butt still stung from the last spanking.

"Bend over," he said pointing to the arm of the sofa.

I obeyed, bracing myself for what was coming. The spanking was hardly anything and I didn't know how to react. All of my sisters knew I was getting another spanking and so after a delay, I figured I better make some noise but the truth was it didn't hurt. The wailing noise I made came out pathetic but it was over with and I stood up facing Dad with a red face more out of embarrassment than out of pain.

Dad rustled my hair and motioned outside and said, "Go!" with just enough of a smile to let me know that he had given me a lot of grace for being disobedient. That grace kept me away from the ditch for the rest of the week.

I think our Heavenly Father is like that with us too. He knows the temptations that we will encounter and he knows that we will fail many of them, but it is His nature to correct those He loves just as a father corrects his son. That being said God expects and warns us to be obedient. It isn't that He is some sort of control freak. He wants life to go well for us. He loves us. After all, He created us, but He created us with "free will" to make decisions through this life in hopes that we will eventually figure it out. He gave us a direction manual if we will just read it. Unfortunately, most of us don't bother to read it and can't figure out why everything seems to fall apart in our life. Much of the trouble that we go through is self-inflicted anyway. The Bible is our manual for Living Life Well. We can read it, but it won't help us unless we apply what it says.

Jesus said that life here on Earth was going to be difficult and it is. But it goes much easier when you are being obedient to His direction. The book of Proverbs is full of wise counsel that teaches us how to make our life run smoother and more successfully. I think one of the most comforting verses in the Bible, for me anyway, is

Proverbs 3:11-12 *"My son, despise not the chastening of the LORD; neither be weary of his correction: For whom the LORD loveth he correcteth; even as a father the son* in whom *he delighteth."*

We all come into this world spoiled wretched children lacking any goodness because God's spirit is not in us. We all have fallen short from birth, spoiled rotten, and self-centered. The Bible says that there is no one that is good. But God, in His mercy gave us a choice to accept the sacrifice of His Son, Jesus, dying on the cross for payment of the natural sin in our life. When we accept that free gift of Jesus through faith, God forgives us with grace. At that point we are filled with the Holy Spirit. The Holy Spirit indwelling in your heart guides you through your life. That is what it means to be born again. If you are born again, you will produce "fruit" by way of the Spirit that indwells you when you accept Jesus.

What is the fruit of the Spirit? It says in Galatians 5:22-23: *"But the fruit of the Spirit is love, joy, peace, longsuffering, gentleness, goodness, faith, Meekness, temperance: against such there is no law."*

 Looking back on that fishing experience can you see the lack of fruit from the Spirit in my life? I deserved another hard spanking for being disobedient to my dad's correction, but he extended my grace with a gentle spanking. Likewise when God has extended grace to you. The grace you don't deserve. It makes you want

26

to be obedient to His instruction. There will come days when you step out of line, and He will correct you. And that is a good thing. It shows you how much He loves you.

It still makes me laugh when I think of Dad putting the sneak on me, barefoot in his undershirt and jeans. I have to wonder what was going through his head. What gets me is how he did it without laughing. Obviously, he was a much better secret spy than I was for sure! The bottom line is, how mad can you get at your child who loves fishing?

SUGGESTED READING:

Ephesians 2:4-10

Proverbs

What is your favorite Proverb?

Snag This:

Can you remember a time when you were disobedient?

Did you get a good spanking?

Have you experienced grace in your life?

Can you see how God's gift of grace would help you to be obedient?

Patience

Dad started us kids fishing as soon as we were able to cast a fishing pole. Our first poles were shorter with a Zebco closed faced reel in the hopes it would alleviate tangled lines and fishing knots. The problem was we were ultimately gifted at tangling our lines into such a convoluted mess it was often easier to cut the line than untangle it. One of Dad's more common statements began with a heavy sigh, and then, "How did this happen?"

I remember having just a hint of pride whenever he asked me that. It implied that he had never seen anything so tangled up in his entire life, and in a warped way there was a sense of accomplishment in such an amazing feat.

Our coordination was challenged from an early age. Walking down a trail without falling down was an accomplishment in itself, but to put a fishing pole in a child's hand was down-right hazardous. It took a lot of courage to lead a small party of little fishermen, loaded with fishing poles down a narrow trail. Someone was bound to get skewered. There is a reason why those large bait bobbers were red and white. It is to warn parents there's a baited hook incoming and they had better duck or get out of the way!

Because Monica was so competitive, she started fishing about the same time I did. Therefore, Dad had two uncoordinated young fishermen he needed to teach. Dad didn't get much fishing done those first few years. He would pick up his pole and almost make a cast about the time one of us would get a knot in our line or hung up in a nearby tree.

"Dad! I need help again." One of us would holler melodiously.

Eventually, Dad pretended that he didn't hear us as he sidetracked around the lake so we would have to figure it out for ourselves. If the mess was really bad Monica and I would help each other. This is when we graduated to an open-faced reel with clear streamline bobbers. The old poles were then handed down to the younger siblings.

During the summer when we were growing up, we pretty much went camping every weekend. Camping trips always included fishing of some sort. Typically we went to one of several favorite spots whether it was fishing the lakes at Trinity Mountain, driving the rough road into Graham Ranger station or camping along the North Fork of the Boise River. Each area held different options. When we fished at Trinity Lakes we brought along the canoes and camped in a designated campground, or we backpacked a short three-mile hike into a remote high mountain lake.

The designated campground meant that there were usually neighbors close by. Now, Dad wasn't a campground kind of guy. He preferred to camp off the beaten path away from noisy neighbors.

The high mountain lake where we backpacked was more Dads' style. It was secluded but it had its challenges as well. I have a snapshot etched into my mind about that particular lake that will never be erased.

Imagine... Dad out front, leading the expedition with his blue backpack and walking stick in hand followed closely by Monica who was unconsciously in competition with everyone. My friend Keith and I were next in line, in our own world conquering the wilderness amongst wildly screaming savages with a pet raccoon crawling between the two of us. Mom brought up the rear encouraging the three youngest girls. Jenny, the middle sister had fallen into a thicket of stinging nettles at the first water crossing. Her shrieks of pain from the wild plant's relentless needle-like sting shattered the serene wilderness. She exited the thicket with arms outstretched covered in swollen red wounds which covered her arms and legs. In an attempt to lighten the mood, Suzanne, the second to the youngest sister, made an overly-dramatic rescue attempt to secure Jenny's backpack which was still lying in the nettle patch. That got Mother and the youngest daughter, Catherine to laugh, which infuriated Jenny who was suffering in extreme pain. Catherine bit her lip trying not to laugh while she optimistically assisted mother who was doing her best to comfort and encourage Jenny to move up the trail. Jenny just wanted to go home. That stinging nettle event overrode any other memory of the backpacking trip although the lake had large cutthroat trout in it. We fished it several years, but we could never get them to bite. A few years later an especially hard winter froze the lake out, killing all of the fish and we never went back.

Ultimately, the all-around favorite camping spot was on the North Fork of the Boise River. Obviously, we called it "Our favorite place" for lack of a better name.

The rugged road down to the unimproved campground was more of a cattle trail to a primitive flat spot next to the river. The river made a sharp turn along a rock face where the river channel had dug out a deep swimming hole on one side and a back eddy circled around depositing a white sandy beach where we camped. The landing itself was peppered with a mixture of mature ponderosa pine and douglas fir trees, an area large enough for three tents and a couple rigs. Dad and Mom had a tent, the four girls slept in a larger one, and I had a tent to myself with the raccoon.

We had these camping excursions down to a routine. Each Friday afternoon when Dad got off work, we loaded up the truck with the wood trailer in tow, and headed up to the mountains to set up camp. Saturday morning Dad and I cut a load of firewood filling the trailer by mid-afternoon. We then returned to camp in time for Dad to take a siesta in the cool shade along the river, and I joined my sisters at the swimming hole. I was sure to keep one eye open for when Dad woke up from his nap knowing that he would be sneaking off to fish in the evening, and I did not want to be left behind.

There were two fishing holes that Dad and I fished during the evening. The first was upstream a couple of hundred yards above a bridge that crossed the river. It was a conspicuous hole where the river ran swiftly down a straight stretch. A clear bobber was difficult to see on the choppy water's surface consequently we had to keep our tips up and reel quickly to keep the line taut. Usually the fish were plentiful here and we typically limited out at this hole. When the fish weren't biting at this spot, we went to a more remote place further up the road.

That spot took a little more work to access. The trail was not as defined. It skirted a swamp hidden amongst tall grass, then wound through thick alder intermixed with spruce before opening up at the base of a high moss-covered rock cliff. Upstream, the river tumbled down a series of rapids cutting along the cliff before plunging into a series of deep holes. Although the water looked quiet and still on the surface, below it swirled powerfully churning from deep within. This stretch of the river did not receive much direct sunlight except when the sun was directly overhead. Consequently, it remained lush green even into August. This hideaway seemed to hold a mysterious secret. The fishing here was quiet, still, and peaceful in the secluded pools at the base of the giant, moss-covered cliff. The narrow obscure trail taught us to maneuver our fishing poles in close quarters and rewarded us with its seclusion by refreshing our spirit.

Looking back on those early years of fishing brings to mind sweet memories of Dad's patience with us while we learned how to fish.

When we are young Christian's first learning about Jesus we are constantly tangling up our lines and getting hung up. God helps us to get going and as we gain our confidence, He tends to stand back, often times remaining silent allowing us to earnestly seek out His direction. That silence helps us to grow in Him. He is still nearby, but He knows the benefits of being silent. It causes us to fellowship with other Christians to help each other grow through various struggles. Struggles are good in that they make us stronger and more resilient. Through all of this, we build a stronger relationship with Him.

We all are gifted in different ways. Some are leaders watching over the flock, competitive members challenge us to grow and move forward. Others are dreamers, visionaries seeking deeper relationships. Those who are hypersensitive to our surroundings signal to the world truths of God even shattering the wilderness with the reality of our dependence on Jesus.

Edifying laughter is always welcome medicine in troubling times, and there are those who bring that beautiful gift in love to lighten life's struggles. Practical people keep us on task with their optimistic no-nonsense outlook. Ultimately, it is all for nothing if we do not have the nurturing love that covers all things.

As we continue in our walk with the Lord, tackling our fast-paced lives tends to slacken our walk, and it is easy to lose sight of the bobber. It is important to keep that line of communication with Him taut. For keeping the line taunt allows us a direct path in life which in turn profits His kingdom. The harvest is ripe, the workers are few and time is short.

There will be seasons in our busy lives when we reach obstacles in our lives, like a cliff seeming to block us from moving on. Those can be scary times and may seem like the Lord is nowhere to be found. It is those times when we stop to seek the Lord off the beaten path, to fast in the quiet stillness where the waters run deep. It is here where we learn about the hidden mysteries of the One who created us. These quiet fasting times replenish our souls giving us direction, purpose and wisdom to make Godly decisions.

Suggested Reading:

1 Corinthians 12:1-11

Mathew 6:1-34

Snag This:

Do you know what spiritual gift you have?

Are you keeping your line of communication tight with the Lord?

Do you ever go somewhere quiet to listen to God's quiet voice?

Have you ever fasted when you needed to make an important decision?

One Long Night

With wide eyes, I viewed the round steaks in the display case. "Pick two of them, one for Friday night and one for Saturday," Dad said, choosing steaks for him and Larry as well. Larry was a college professor Dad knew from Oregon State University. He was a good friend and would be joining us on this annual backpacking trip. Dad and Larry had been backpacking together for years. This was my second annual ten-day backpacking trip and being eleven years old if asked I was pretty much an expert.

Strategically shopping and packing for the excursion into the backcountry was just about as exciting as the trip itself. One of the steaks was wrapped together with the unfrozen one before rolling both of them together in the bottom of a sleeping bag to keep them cold during the hike. The frozen one kept the first night's steak refrigerated and was thawed out by the second night. After we had eaten the steak on the second night, we were on our own. We would need to live off the land which meant catching fish for dinner. We split up packing the pancake mix, dried soup mix, cheese slices, bread, summer sausage and squeeze butter between the four of us. All of the other items, space food sticks, granola bars and dried Tang juice packages, we were responsible for ourselves.

Dad tossed his old orange backpacking tent to me and said, "You better take this in case it rains." Larry had his single tent and Dad had just got a new tent and there was not enough room for Keith, Dad and me in it. "You and Keith can sleep in this one."

Keith was the next door neighbor. He was a year younger than me, and we did almost everything together. This was his first extended backpacking trip. It was the middle of August so I laughed at Dad and stated "That's way too heavy. Besides, it's summertime. It's not going to rain."

Keith picked up the tent, checked the weight, and nodded in agreement. At eleven years old we were both, all about packing light.

"Okay, it's up to you, but if it rains, you're not sleeping in my tent!" Dad warned.

Contemplating the consequences I looked at Keith and then outside at the clear blue sky. I had a strange feeling in my gut to reconsider, but ignored it with all of the excitement of packing. There were more important things to pack like a wrist rocket and the new 35mm Nikon camera Dad had given me for my birthday.

Dad showed me how to load the film into the new camera and gave me two rolls of 36 exposure black and white film. The two aluminum film containers had Kodak orange lids screwed onto them. The containers in my hands were as precious as gold. I dreamed of the photos that I would take rivaling the ones in the latest subscriptions of National Geographic and Life magazines. He gave me specific instructions to shoot sparingly.

The initial hike up the valley floor towards the Big Horn Crags was easy. Keith and I charged out ahead ready to conquer the wilderness with an abundant amount of energy. Dad reminded us several times to pace ourselves whenever we stopped and waited for him and Larry to catch up. We agreed happily before racing off on the next stretch when the trail was abruptly intercepted by abundant white-water gushing down across the trail in its long journey to the ocean. Milling around the crossing, we searched for a log to cross but could not find one. When Dad and Larry got there, Dad suggested that we take off our boots and socks to cross barefoot. Keith and I followed their lead, tucking our socks into our boots, tying the long laces together and draping them over our neck. Dad led the crossing party, and Larry brought up the rear.

The icy water produced an involuntary sucking whistle sound from my lips trapping an intense amount of oxygen into my system. I assumed it was an involuntary reaction my body produced for self-preservation. I had remembered reading something about this in biology the previous year. I figured that I was too young yet to produce a howl like Dad was doing ahead of me. The shock had blinded a majority of my bodily functions. By mid-stream, my feet were completely numb, and I could not feel the rocks with my bare toes. It quickly became apparent that both Keith and I had not rolled up our pants far enough. Desperately holding on to a walking stick, I was committed to maintaining my balance against the force of the icy water racing down from the snow drifts high above us. Visions of early pioneers who had died in river crossings at high water came to mind and made sense now.

I was able to exhale upon reaching the bank on the other side but not before floaties danced in front of my eyes. I figured I had better sit down before I fell down due to lack of oxygen, numbness in my legs or a combination of both. All feeling had escaped from my cold red feet, and I rubbed them furiously to dry them before putting my socks and boots back on. Looking back at the crossing I made a mental note to consider throwing my backpack across and trying to jump the six-foot stream on the way back.

Recovering quickly, we resumed our trek to our first night's destination. Soon the trail became steeper, sapping any extra energy Keith and I had. In no time we were far behind Dad and Larry. Each trudging step produced small puffs of dust lifting us inch by inch from the valley floor. We shed our long sleeved shirts revealing our white t-shirts as the heat of the afternoon sun beat down on us. We longed for a spring coming out of the rocks to quench our thirst. The backpacks grew heavier as we worked our way up the steep trail to the high mountain lake nestled amongst the granite peaks.

With a triumphant whoop, Dad and Larry disappeared from sight ahead of us. Knowing the high mountain lake was in sight, a surge of adrenaline shot through Keith and I, eliminating the strain of the steep trail, and we scrambled the last leg of the ascent anxious to get a glimpse of the crystal blue, high mountain lake. Dad and Larry had already settled on a camping spot and were standing at the lake's edge surveying the potential for fishing. By the time Keith and I reached the camping spot, they had begun setting up their tents. Since Keith and I didn't have a tent to set up we scrambled to assemble our fishing gear. Dad informed us that we needed to get enough firewood gathered for the night and the next morning before we could go fishing. We scanned the lake for any sign of fish rising as we gathered the wood. Keith spotted a fish hitting the surface of the lake, prompting both of us to get the firewood chore done at a breakneck speed.

Dad had a plastic box in which he kept a wide variety of dry flies. He gave both Keith and I a demonstration on how to tie the fly on the leader that went to the back of a clear streamline bobber. About three feet ahead of the bobber, he tied a shorter leader that would dangle down dancing in the water ahead of the bobber. I chose a Joe's Grasshopper for the back and a Mosquito for the front.

Upon completion of the tutorial, Keith and I headed for the lake in a competition to see who would land the first cutthroat. Dad hollered after us to be careful not to lose those flies in the trees. Counting down to three, we cast our lines out simultaneously in great anticipation. A thick twelve-inch cutthroat swam up to my front fly. The water was so clear it was difficult to tell when the fish was at the fly and I set the hook prematurely causing the fish to miss the fly altogether. Frustrated, the brightly colored fish wheeled around striking the back fly with fury and the line went taut. Hooked securely, the wild trout dove deep in the water fighting furiously and then shot towards the surface jumping out of the water with the clear bobber trailing close behind. Within seconds Keith reported a fish on with laughter and the competition switched to the biggest and the most. Dad hearing all of the commotion appeared on the shoreline wearing his fishing vest and an old dilapidated straw hat of sorts which had been smashed down by years of backpacking trips. A multitude of flies of every size and color was hooked into the band of the flattened hat. Dad smoked Roitan Banker Cigars when he fished, and although the fishing vest might camouflage his location, the plume of whitish grey smoke gave his location away. His laughter carried across the high mountain lake with each fish he caught.

Searching around the lake I could not spot Larry. Larry wasn't much of a fisherman. He preferred capturing the wilderness experience on his camera. It took some time, but I eventually spotted his tall slender profile in a meadow over by camp in his trademarked off-white backpacking slacks. He was on his hands and knees clutching his Nikon camera only inches away from an unsuspecting wildflower. He and dad had multiple lenses for their Nikon cameras, and it was not unusual to catch them off the trail taking a photo of something unique that had captured their eye. Since both of them were fascinated with geology and glaciology, Keith and I were often used as a reference for size against a polished glacial scar traversing a granite slope or a rogue avalanche chute with uprooted trees in the background.

Dad called us from camp as the shadows grew long. Smoke signaled that it would soon be supper time and Dad appointed Keith and me to cut willows to cook the steaks on. We both had sharp hunting knives on our belts and carried them proudly. We had taken great care in sharpening them before the trip. It was a badge of honor to have our parents entrust us with such a weapon graduating us into the elite echelon of mountain men. As any mountain man knew, there was an art to cutting willows to cook a chunk of steak on. They needed to be long enough to keep the person cooking away from the searing heat of the coals. Strong enough at the tip to support a mouthful of juicy steak and green enough that it would not burn through. If the stick burnt through, the steak portion inevitably fell into the fire which induced frantic pandemonium. This instantaneously transformed a once civilized backpacker into a primitive savage stabbing wildly at the chunk of steak buried in the hot coals. In the event that the rescue attempt was successful the primal being would grunt inconspicuously while flicking the larger pieces of ash from the meat before wildly tearing at it with their teeth. Cutting willows was a responsibility not to be taken lightly.

Dad was an exquisite backcountry chef. The first two nights of the trip we ate well fueling us to forge onto other high mountain lakes speckled throughout this mountain range. Fish were plentiful in the lakes where we camped giving us a surge of optimism for the five upcoming steakless suppers.

On our fourth night after an extra difficult day of hiking, we camped at a lake that held a lot of promise. Upon reaching the lake, Keith and I went on a recon mission to see what the lake held in relation to dinner. We reported back excitedly that there was not a multitude of fish but what we saw were large! By this time we all knew our roles and quickly got the chores finished.

As we fished, the skies began to darken. It looked and even smelled like a thunderstorm was brewing. Dad informed Keith and I that we had better prepare for a night of rain since we didn't have a tent. Keith and I went through the options that were at hand. We could build a shelter with poles and pine boughs or find a natural shelter to keep us dry for the night and out of the weather. Time was not on our side so the optimum choice was to find natural shelter and build off of it. One thing was certain; we had to do this with little complaint as to not show Dad that he had been right as usual.

We surveyed the materials at hand. Our camp location was at timberline so trees were limited, and this far up on the mountain, they had the potential to be lightning rods anyway. There was a boulder field on one side of the lake a couple of hundred yards from camp. One large boulder was propped up by a couple of smaller boulders on each side leaving an empty space in between. The boulders were nestled next to a small grassy meadow so we decided to investigate. As we approached the boulder field we caught glimpses of movement darting in and out. Upon further investigation, it became apparent that a colony of small chinchilla looking rodents resided in the boulder field. I knew of these high mountain rock dwellers from past hiking trips, and they were actually on my bucket list of "things to catch". The furry little rodent was called a Pika. The high mountain dwellers lived in these rocks year round and survived by harvesting grasses from the small meadows and drying them on the rocks in the sun. These haystacks could get quite large and were what they lived on during the long cold winters.

Upon further analysis of the large boulder, we optimistically noted that two boys about our size could fit under it, though quite uncomfortably. Other large rocks next to our fortress offered refuge to stash our backpacks out of the weather. Keith and I were masters at fort building and we set to task to make it our domain by spreading the already present haystacks into a sleeping area. As we worked, Pika nearby peeped much to our delight. I envisioned catching one of the cute little rodents before the end of the trip.

When we were finished we stood back admiring our new living quarters. Dad and Larry smiled at us upon our report that we had secured shelter under the giant rock. Dad was excited to come over to inspected our new fortress. He looked it over carefully and I knew he was probably envious but didn't want to let on. He warned us that if we heard rocks tumbling above us to make a mad dash for camp. I looked up on the steep mountain towering back behind us as a large raindrop hit my arm. Keith and I scrambled to get our packs out of the rain and get set up under the rock. The rain came down in buckets all evening and into the night. We didn't dare venture out for fear of getting completely drenched in the torrential downpour. Hunger and boredom quickly set in as we laid in our sleeping bags. We were dry; however, the roof above us was quite low confining us strictly to our sleeping bags. To curb our appetites we ate a couple of our space food sticks and a breakfast bar reasoning that we would surely be able to catch fish for breakfast when the thunderstorm passed. As evening turned into night the peeping of the Pika became somewhat annoying. They were relentless and peeping from all directions.

Suddenly the landscape lit up the entire lake with a thunderous KABOOM rocking the mountain sending a series of echoes rattling down the valleys below. Both Keith and I held our breath listening intently for rocks that might fall down the mountain entombing us with the wild rodents.

By the middle of the night, the lightning had moved further down the mountain range, but we now faced a new danger. Somewhere through the raging storm we became covered in total darkness, and surrounded by Pika. Our well developed imagination took over, transforming the once gentle creatures into vicious bloodthirsty rodents. Plus they had substantially increased in size. We would begin to doze off when a large Pika would signal another one to move in for the kill causing us to sit up in a defensive position singing out loud. Singing loudly seemed to keep them at bay. We were obligated to sing most of the night, the same song, over and over and over. Who would have thought that singing Roger Miller's rendition of "King of the Road" could deter giant Pika?

It was about that time when I felt something in the haystack I was laying on jabbing me in my side. Initially I thought it was a stick protruding from the haystack material, but the more I thought about it, I had to wonder if it was actually a rib bone left over from other unsuspecting mountain men. These vicious animals had probably lured them into their dens only to torture them to death with their incessant peeping and gnashing fangs. As the night wore on exhaustion prevailed, and we fell asleep just as the horizon lightened in the east.

Daylight spread quickly across the landscape and the giant Pika receded back to small creatures retreating into their underground dens to wait for a more opportune time. With stomachs growling, Keith and I crawled from our fortress and made our way to the campfire where Dad was warming water for coffee and hot chocolate. Dad smiled at the two of us on our approach. "How was your night?" he asked.

"Not bad," Keith answered, yawning. I just stared at the smoke rising from the fire, totally exhausted from battling the enemy all night, humming King of the Road. I have always packed a tent since.

We all have those sleepless nights where our problems become bigger than life, continuously haunting us all night long. Where is that money going to come from? How is that bill going to be paid? What are we going to do if such and such happens? The bottom line is most of what we worry about doesn't come to pass and what we worry about always seems to work itself out one way or another.

Jesus had quite a bit to say about worrying in Matthew 6: 34 *"Take therefore no thought for the morrow: for the morrow shall take thought for the things of itself. Sufficient unto the day* is *the evil thereof."*

Suggested Reading

Matthew 6:25-34

Psalm 23

Snag This:

Have you lost sleep due to fear or worry?

Were you able to change anything the more you worried?

Did things seem better during the daylight?

Have you tried laying down your troubles to the Lord?

The Man Purse

"Man, I don't want to go to the pep assembly today," I said pulling into the parking lot at school. "Look at this!" spreading my arms out at the clear blue sky, green grass, and budding trees. "It's a beautiful spring day. We should be fishing today."

"Me either." Nick replied "What's this assembly for anyway? Basketball season is over. "

"Some student council thing, ughhhh," I said dramatically sticking my tongue out and rolling my eyes.

"Hey, let's skip it! We can go to first period and then we can sneak out after we have made our presence known!" Nick said slamming the heavy door to the '64 International pickup.

I looked across the hood of the truck at Nick to see how serious he was. It was Friday and we only had half a day, plus it was our senior year. We were getting close to graduation and both of us were ready for school to be done. We had serious short-timer syndrome.

The last time we skipped, we bought a beat-up '55 Chevy four-door for a measly $50 bucks and just about got busted. We got out of that deal by the skin of our teeth, and even sold it for $75 after we took it hill climbing all day! But still, that was a close call getting pulled over for a bad brake light!

"Okay, but I think I'll see if I can get Monica to write a note just in case," I said. "I am sure she is hanging around Kyle's locker."

We walked down the hall and sure enough, there was my sister, Monica.

"Hey, can you write us a note to miss the pep assembly?" I whispered to her.

"Oh man! You guys are going to get us in trouble one of these days!" She said in a lecturing tone.

"Well, I can't write it myself or we will get in trouble for sure!" I replied.

"What are you going to do?" Monica asked getting the paper out of her notebook.

"We're going fishing," I said under my breath. "We'll be back in time for supper."

Monica rolled her eyes dramatically as she wrote the note. "What are you going to do with the fish, if you catch any?" she asked.

"I don't know. Release them I guess" I replied and thought, *"Man, she always asked such good questions."*

"Well be careful," she said handing me the note. "Seems like all I do is pray for you!"

"Thanks, you're awesome!" I said, smiling at her.

Nick and I met in the parking lot as planned after first period. His metallic green '58 Chevy pickup was parked right next to my 64 International, so the transfer was easy.

The dark green International pickup had a silver homemade camper with two doors that opened into the back. There was a bed against the cab and cupboards along the sides along the top. Nick was transferring an army green canvas fishing creel that he kept his tackle in. "What is that?" I asked sarcastically.

"It's a creel," he said with a big sigh, checking to make sure he had everything he needed in it. It had a shoulder strap and even a ruler printed on the side with pockets for various types of tackle. If you happened to catch any fish you could carry them in the large pocket.

"It looks like a man purse," I said.

Nick responded with a look of contempt. "It's not a man purse. It's a creel."

"Just sayin, looks like a man purse to me," I said, not giving up on harassing him. Nick and I were best friends, more like brothers actually. He had one sister with no brothers and I had four sisters without a brother so we naturally gave each other a bad time anytime the opportunity arose.

Nick ignored me moving his fishing pole and extra coat from behind the seat of his truck. Suddenly, I spotted Calhoun, the campus cop, turn in at the far end of the parking lot.

"Crap! There's Calhoun. We better keep a low profile." Nick and I both ducked and jumped in the camper and shut the door. We were never too concerned about Calhoun. He couldn't catch a cold even if his life depended on it.

Patiently we watched Calhoun patrol the parking lot before driving around the building and out of sight. As soon as the cop car went around the corner, Nick and I jumped out of the camper and into the cab. Nick ducked down in the seat so no one would see both of us leave the school together. I drove out of the parking lot with the window down and my arm out the window as casual as I could. We took the back roads skirting town as a precaution and headed north towards Highway 55.

"Where should we go?" Nick asked.

"I don't know. Anywhere is better than being stuck in that assembly!" I said.

We drove with no particular destination in mind up Highway 55 through the small town of Horseshoe Bend north along the Payette River. The river was high and murky with the spring runoff in full swing so we decided to head up the South Fork of the Payette at Banks towards Lowman.

We were both itching to get some fishing in and randomly picked one of the first turnouts on the winding highway along the stretch of river called Staircase. Staircase was a series of rapids that worked up the river like stair steps. They were steep and were class IV rapids for rafters and kayakers. The odds of a fish being able to survive the Staircase rapids was minimal, but that did not hinder our optimism. There was a large rock sitting in the middle of Staircase appropriately named House Rock. Typically the rushing water ran on either side of the rock but this time of year water was rushing over the top of it by several feet. The warm spring weather was melting the snow rapidly in the high country, and all of the rivers were swollen, etching new high water marks in the banks.

I always had a pole set up and ready to go fishing. I never knew when I might need to stop and throw a line out. There was a tube container inside the camper that ran alongside the bed which my fishing pole slid into. I had learned early on that the first one to cast into the hole usually hooked the fish so I wasted no time climbing down the bank to a large rock angling down into the tumultuous water. There was a small back eddy close to shore just downstream from a large boulder. I had seen it from the road and figured that it held one of the largest fish on the Payette River, and I was going to hook it before Nick had his fishing pole rigged up. Nick was notoriously late on everything; whether it was hunting, school or in this case fishing.

I was quite proud of myself for getting to the big rock first and climbed up on top of it scanning my newly acclaimed territory. It took some time to steady myself on the peak of the rock because it angled down quite sharply. The rock was about eight foot wide and twice as long plunging into the icy water. Teetering in position, I struggled to steady myself before attempting to cast my black and white Mepps spinner. When I shifted my feet to get a better angle to hit the small eddy, both feet slipped out from underneath me and I landed squarely on my butt, and began sliding swiftly down the rock. The cold water from the rapids had splashed up onto the rock and froze overnight leaving a thin layer of ice across the rock face. Instinctively, I quickly tossed my pole to the bank, rolling over on my stomach, and spreading myself out while digging my boots and my fingernails into the solid slick granite slab. I slid about seven feet down the giant rock sensing at any second I would run out of rock and plunge into the torrential current. Many thoughts raced through my mind with the main one being, there would be no way I could survive the cold water dodging the many boulders with the swift current. In no time hypothermia would set in and there wasn't a person alive who could survive swimming in that swift water without a life preserver.

Incredibly I caught an edge with my boot, and came to a stop. Ever so carefully I looked up to the truck parked on the road above. Nick was at the back of the truck still rigging up his fishing pole unaware of the predicament I had got myself into.

When I hollered, "Nick!" the force of me hollering knocked my foot loose and I started sliding further down the rock.

Crap! He couldn't hear me over the roar of the rapids. My heart was racing and I fought full-blown panic.

My fingers dug desperately into the rock as gravity pulled my body over the rough granite slab. Unexpectedly my right toe caught a sharp edge stopping me. I searched frantically with my hands and found two small indentions that I clung to for dear life. I felt the ice slowly melt away under my fingers and the rough surface of the granite added substance to hold on to. I was thankful that my Levis had bunched up and were additionally helping me cling to the rock. Cool mist from a nearby rapid hit my bare right leg. I knew that the toe dug into the hard rock surface was merely inches from where the rock and the river met. Daring not to move one iota, I tried my best to calm down and carefully took a deep breath. With everything in me I hollered, "Hey!" while trying desperately not to move my body.

I didn't budge that time and Nick turned to look down at me. My face was turned up looking towards the truck with my cheek pressed hard into the cold rock. Nick focused on me and I could see the terror in his eyes. He dropped his pole and I hollered "Get a rope!"

Nick raced around the truck searching frantically for anything that he could use to help me. My fingers were growing weak, and I was afraid that I wouldn't be able to hold on much longer.

"Hurry!"

I heard him scrambling down the rock bank. He was out of my line of sight until he climbed up to the top of the rock, eight feet above me.

"I couldn't find a rope." He said out of breath. He climbed onto the rock and stretched his body as far as he dared to go. His reach was still a good three feet away.

"I don't think you can reach me Nick, with your hand," I whispered. I was thankful someone was now close enough to talk to. I looked down the rock to the churning water only inches from my foot.

"Yeah, I know," Nick said, "Grab a hold of this."

Out of the corner of my eye, I saw him flop something down the rock towards me.

My eyes strained to look up towards what he threw and saw with utter horror my demise that lay before me. I expected any second my life would flash before me. The *man purse* lay inches from my right hand.

My heart sank in my chest, *"Really?"* I let out a big sigh.

Nick said, "Grab hold, I've got you."

"Boy, talk about going from bad to worse!" I thought. The creel was four inches from my fingers. This was going to take total commitment to release what I clung to for dear life, to a lifeline I wasn't so sure I trusted.

I strained to look at Nick with uncertainty in my eyes. "Are you sure?"

"Grab hold, I promise. I won't let go." Nick reassured me.

I let out another sigh, "Okay..."

I closed my eyes and said, *"Please help me,"* under my breath.

I whispered, "One, two, three" and lunged forward grabbing the creel. Once I felt it in my hands and saw that it held me, the tension in my body gradually relaxed.

Now it was just a matter of persistent perseverance to work my way up the rock face. Nick kept constant pressure on the creel, and I pushed with my toes and body wriggling an inch at a time.

We both collapsed next to each other when I cleared the top of the rock.

"Wow, that was a rush!" Nick said looking over at me.

"Yeah, it was!" I replied, "We need to find a better fishing spot!"

I looked at Nick's creel and shook my head. "Who'd a thought that could have saved me?"

It's just like that with us and God you know? We go through life getting ourselves in trouble making poor choices. When we get into a bind we call on God. "Oh Lord please help us!" He moves near to us, and we feel all warm and secure when we are talking to Him but are we really sincere? We make promises and when He gets us out of trouble, we tend to forget about Him. Have we really reached out and fully committed? In order to really commit, we have to drop everything that gives us security however unstable that is and latch on with all that we have to His promise.

Because we cannot see Him, we have to trust in the promise that is in His word. That is what makes it so scary. It takes faith. Faith in something we cannot see. For some of us, it takes a huge amount of faith but when we grab on to His promise with everything we have, it doesn't take long to see that there is security in it. We still need to wriggle our way through the trials of this life, but with His steady hand to guide us and His unfailing word we will be blessed with eternal life. That blessed assurance is all the security needed and is a much better spot to be.

Before I asked Jesus into my life I used to look at Christians as weak. It wasn't until I began to get into the Word, and walk the walk when I saw how wrong I had been. To take a stand for what God says in His Word takes faith. That faith walking through trials produces confidence in Jesus who provides salvation eternally. That is why Jesus said that the gate is small and the path is narrow. Not many are willing to walk the walk. With His firm grip He helps us work through the struggles of this life, and lead us to an eternal award!

Suggested Reading:

Deuteronomy 3:18

Joshua 1:5

Revelation 3:19-22

Snag This:

Have you ever got yourself in a serious predicament?

Did you call out to the Lord for help?

Did it change your life afterwards or did you go back to your old ways?

Have you let go of *everything* and reached out for Him?

What are some worldly things you are still holding on to?

Potatoes and Onions

The last 94# lb bag of Portland cement caused the truck to drop an inch when it hit the bed. I nodded to the driver and waved, "Thanks! Have a great weekend!" Then I turned to Rob.

"Yeah, I have no plans for anything this weekend. I will probably go fishing somewhere."

"We should go backpacking into the Spanish Peaks!" Rob said excitedly. "My wife is gone for the weekend visiting her sister, and I have the whole weekend to myself!"

"I am broke, and payday isn't until next week." I retorted. I had only been working at the brickyard for a week and that first paycheck was already spoken for.

Rob was not dissuaded easily. "Dude, what's it going to cost? I have a few potatoes and an onion. We can catch fish to eat. It will be an inexpensive weekend!"

"That is true," I thought. The trailhead was less than an hour away. I had enough gas in the truck to get there and back and the thought of fishing high mountain lakes was extremely appealing. It would be much more enjoyable than sitting at home over the long Labor Day weekend. On top of that, I would learn some new country around my new home in Bozeman.

Rob's dark brown hair hung over his ears with day-old stubble on his ruddy face. His bright, brown eyes waited in anticipation for my answer. Rob's energy level exceeded normal on everything. I had only known him a few days since I started work at the brickyard. He was one of the first people from back east that I had met in my conservative 19 years of life. His tan slacks and horizontal striped polo shirt along with the slick bottomed warehouse loafers was the first thing that caught my attention when I met him. He seemed like a big city guy. I wondered what a trip into the back country of Montana would look like with him. We had gone fishing earlier in the week on the property he and his wife rented along a remote stretch of West Fork of the Gallatin River. He had fishing down pat and had out-fished me landing some lunker browns causing me to withhold any preconceived judgment on him. I desperately wanted to fish that stretch of the river again using the technique he had shared with me. I needed to appease that relationship in order to do so. "Okay, what the heck!"

I dropped him off at the entrance to his long driveway making arrangements to leave first thing the next morning. Between the two of us, we figured that we had three potatoes, an onion, a partial tub of margarine, half a loaf of bread and a few tea bags. We would eat like kings!

There were several rigs in the trailhead parking lot with out of state plates along with a few local Montana outfits with horse trailers attached.

Neither one of us had a map on hand so we made a mental note of the trail system from an interpretive sign of the Spanish Peaks Wilderness Area. Rob wanted to climb to the top of one of the highest peaks. I looked at that peak from the parking lot and noticed on the north face there was a long finger of snow still attached to the steep mountain. I marked in my mind the lakes to fish on our ascent. There was another interpretive sign warning about grizzlies in the area. The sign showed visual differences comparing grizzlies to black bears.

The first three miles were easy hiking giving the misleading impression that this was going to be a piece of cake. Before long, the trail steepened causing my legs to burn and my heart to pound loudly. Sweat formed on my forehead working into my eyes, and dripped off the end of my nose.

Rob, like a salmon going through the rapids, raced up the hill. The steeper it got the faster he went. I, on the other hand, wondered if he had put rocks in my pack. It didn't take long before Rob was out of sight. I slowed down to enjoy the hike, stopping to shoot photos whenever the opportunity arose. I savored the smell of the evergreens and lush vegetation on the north facing slope and even the sweet smell of the occasional horse manure brought back memories of growing up in Idaho.

I couldn't resist the large thick thimbleberries growing alongside the trail, and slowed to pick a handful here and there. The bushes were loaded with them, and I was thankful that Rob was running up the trail to spook any feeding grizzlies. I caught a glimpse of his orange and brown striped polo shirt on a switchback up ahead, and set that point in my mind to stop and get a drink of water.

I put my head down with determination watching for horse manure and protruding rocks that might cause me to trip when I heard a strange sound ahead of me. I looked up to see a lady sitting on a rock on the side of the trail sobbing.

She jumped and gasped when I said, "Hi."

Her sitting there startled me, and her sobbing unnerved me even more. I searched for a place in the steep trail where I could stop near her.

"Hello", she said through muffled sobs frantically wiping tears from her cheeks with a flowered handkerchief.

"Are you okay?" I asked.

"I am lost!" she sobbed, her shoulders dropped in despair.

I sat down on a log across from her, and pulled my backpack off, propping it up against the rock behind me.

"Well, that's too bad!" I said. "Are you up here by yourself?"

"No, my friends are up here too, but I don't know where they are," she said.

She had regained her composure and was tucking her handkerchief in the front pocket of her tan shorts. She wore a red tank top, and I could tell that she was getting cold. It was cool in the shade, and gosebumps were popping up on her pale arms and legs.

"I am sure they are up at the lake." I reassured her, "You will find them when you get there."

As I got a drink of water, I surveyed her demeanor. She was a thirty-something year old woman and a little homely. She dressed like an environmentalist from somewhere back east, and could have been a cover girl for an eastern backpacker catalog. Her nose was disproportionately large, and her pale skin was quite striking. Her dishwater blond hair was braided into pigtails so tight that they curved upward at the ends. She wore no make-up so the red around her eyes and nose from sobbing stood out even more against her light skin. She spoke with a whining mid-west accent, which just about made the hair on the back of my neck stand up. I tried not to think it, but wondered if her friends had put some distance between her on purpose. I noticed Rob sure hadn't stuck around.

I introduced myself and she said, "Nice to meet you, Bill. My name is Evelyn."

I was tucking my water bottle away in my backpack when a squirrel ran across the trail a few feet from us. Evelyn leaped towards me in a frantic attempt to get away from the passing rodent. Her blood-curdling scream made me gasp as well, and her lunging towards me made me react in momentary hysteria, sending a surge of terror coursing through my body.

"Well, that cleared out this portion of Montana!" I thought, doing my best to recover from the shock.

She started to cry again. Her handkerchief protruded from between her white knuckles. "I hate it up here!" She sobbed.

I grabbed for my backpack and said, "C'mon, let's go find your friends."

She scrambled frantically to get her backpack on and get to her feet. It was certain that she was not going to be left behind again. Evelyn was obviously not used to walking on a trail and stumbled often. She walked so close behind me I was concerned that she might fall on me which pushed us swiftly up the trail. By the time we got to the lake, she had dropped back offering me a little breathing room. I figured the altitude was getting the better of her, and slowed the pace to help her out.

When I walked up to Rob he looked at me and rolled his eyes, shaking his head. I followed his eyes back to the lady and tried not to laugh; she was dragging her backpack across the meadow by the shoulder strap. I set my pack down against a log surveying the lake for any sign of her friends.

" Yeah, she's not having a good day," I said quietly.

I was relieved to see smoke coming from a campsite on the other side of the lake, and was pretty sure that would be her friends. When I turned back to Evelyn she was sitting on her backpack in the middle of the meadow, and she was crying again. I went over and as comforting as I could suggest that she stay here and I would go see if I could find her friends.

As I neared the campfire on the other side of the lake, I noticed they had horses and mules tethered to a high-line. This was not her party. There was an 'ol Montana boy firing up his cook stove in a wall tent. The rest of the party was out fishing.

"Have you guys had any luck?" I asked.

"Nope" he answered with a grin. "I think this lake has freshwater shrimp in it, so they're not biting what we are offering."

I relayed the lady's story to the older gentlemen and asked him if he had seen anyone else up around the lake.

He shook his head while reassuring, "I am sure they will show up soon looking for her. I would just sit tight."

I agreed, and thanking him headed the rest of the way around the lake to survey any potential fishing spots.

When I got back to camp, Evelyn had her backpack propped against a giant boulder and was in a fierce battle with a swarm of mosquitoes. It appeared that she was losing. Rob was on his knees, bent over, with his face close to a pile of sticks nurturing a bright red coal. A large plume of gray smoke began to billow up from the handful of twigs Rob was blowing on and suddenly a flame appeared which helped brighten Evelyn's spirits.

I relayed the unfortunate news about her friends to Evelyn, and was surprised how well she received it. She didn't cry but a defiant look grew in her eyes staring into the fire's dancing flames. I figured she was tired of being scared, and was now madder than a wet hen. It was a significant improvement, but caused me to exercise caution nonetheless. That intense glare could prove to be unpredictable.

I kept one eye on her while I set up my backpacking tent. Evelyn retrieved an olive green sweater from her pack and put it on. Then she pulled her knees up to her chest and stretched the sweater over her knees in an attempt to protect her bare legs from the marauding mosquitoes. I could only imagine what was going on in the poor woman's mind. I assumed that she was pretty scared having been abandoned by her friends, and humiliated by being forced to camp with strangers in this Montana wilderness. She was intently watching Rob tend to the fire. I thought it was interesting how Rob had given her such wide berth. After all, they had both come from back east somewhere. I would have thought they would have acted more neighborly. Folks from back east were sure interesting.

Once Rob had the fire going strong, he announced that he was going to try to catch some fish for dinner. I told him I would join him soon, and Evelyn repositioned herself closer to the fire.

I asked Evelyn if she had any long pants that she could put on because it was going to get cold as soon as the sun went over the ridge. She said that she did in her pack, but then hesitated. Looking around the forest in complete bewilderment, she asked where she could change. I looked around and said, "Well, there is a changing room on the back side of every tree."

From the distinct sneer on her face, I sensed that option was off the table so I offered for her to use my tent to change in.

I grabbed her pack to move it closer to the tent and was shocked at how much it weighed. "What in the world do you have in this thing?" I asked.

"I know! It's heavy, huh? My *friends* divided everything up and put all of the food in my pack, but they have the tent!"

"Oh really?" I laughed, "Imagine that!"

I told her that she could go ahead and sleep in my tent, and I would sleep under the stars tonight. I looked up at the clear Montana sky. It was going to be a beautiful night. That seemed to lighten her mood and replied, "Well, you two are going to eat well tonight because I am not packing this food back, and *my friends* are going to pay dearly for abandoning me!"

Rob was putting a swivel on his line, and I caught a smile on his face when he turned and headed to the lake. I knew what he was thinking... all the pressure was off on the fishing!

And I was thinking, "good thing because if that 'ol boy on the other side of the lake was correct, we were stuck eating spuds and onions for dinner.

The line whirred off of my spinning reel as the clear streamlined bobber sailed out and into the high mountain lake. There was a resounding "klonk" as it hit the water, echoing off the rock walls of the glacial cirque. The splash shattered the perfectly mirrored reflection sending a myriad of ripples streaming across the still water. Anticipation of the first cast built up inside of me as I ever so slowly reeled the line in keeping the tip up and the line taut. I watched with high hopes as a cruising fourteen-inch cutthroat wheeled around to inspect the mosquito fly delicately dancing ahead of the bobber. The large trout eyed the front fly with not so much as a glance, and with a switch of its tail swam towards the black knat on the back leader before disappearing into the middle of the deep lake.

Each cast produced similar results. It seemed as though the 'ol Montana man was correct about the lake being infested with fresh water shrimp. The fish were just not willing to strike at flies or lures. The last remaining rays of the sun disappeared quickly off of the granite mountain backdrop which tripped the switch on the temperature as well. By the time we got back to camp, Rob and I welcomed the roar of the fire Evelyn had stoked which produced an orange glow about the camp. I was quite impressed with the amount of wood she had gathered. I wondered if that was out of fear of wild animals or the fear of getting cold. Her temperament was warmer too. I noticed that she had her long pants on and there was something else different about her too. I tried not to be overly obvious when I did a double take. She looked much better than when we had left, and I had to wonder if she had put on makeup or maybe it was just the fragrance of the food cooking she was preparing.

Evelyn redeemed herself with our fishless dinner. It seems that her friends were quite well prepared and very impressive gourmet outdoor chefs to boot. The meals had all been pre-made and wrapped in aluminum foil. All she had to do was throw the packages on a hot bed of coals for about fifteen minutes, and we ate like royalty with sourdough rolls on the side and even individually wrapped blackberry pie for dessert. After dinner, we had a cup of hot chocolate. The flickering flames from the fire brought out the best in Rob's personality too. Both he and Evelyn relaxed and laughter came easy. I could tell that Evelyn felt like she was part of the group now.

As the fire slowly died down to a bed of coals, the Montana sky lit up with the Milky Way. We each laid on our back gazing up at the stars commenting in great delight at the occasional shooting star racing across the midnight sky. Evelyn offered for me to share the tent with her, but I figured it was best to sleep out under the stars that night. I knew she was frightened to be out there in the wilderness, and I did my best to reassure her that she was all right.

Early the next morning sunlight somehow made its way through the sleeping bag covers which were pulled tightly over my head. The mosquitoes had finally given up on their feeding frenzy sometime during the night. I laid there watching the sunlight work down from the top of Lone Mountain transforming the large mountain into solid gold. Birds sang loudly around camp when I heard a splash out in the lake. *"Maybe the fish were biting now!"* I wondered.

I quickly pulled on my pants and sweatshirt, and put on my socks and boots. Rob heard me rustle out of my sleeping bag, and poked his head out, opening one sleepy eye with the other closed tight.

"I think I heard a fish jump!" I reported.

Rob retreated back into his sleeping bag mumbling something about getting up soon, and rolled over.

I had fished my way around the lake without as much as a bite when I noticed the 'ol Montana man working his way around the lake towards me. He had a speckled blue tin cup of coffee in his hand instead of a fishing pole.

"Having any luck?" he hollered.

I shook my head and said, "Nope, I think you were right about those freshwater shrimp!"

"What happened with that gal?" He asked, "Did her friends ever show up?"

I continued to fish while talking to the gray-haired man. He had a twinkle in his eye when he spoke, and a contagious smile that made you wonder what he was up to. I couldn't help but like him.

"Nope, never saw hide nor hair of anybody last night, but she sure cooked a mean supper!" I replied.

I told him about how they had her pack all of the food, and he got quite a chuckle out of that. "Serves them right, leaving her alone up here." He said.

The man set his cup down on a rock and was digging in his shirt for a package of tobacco with one hand. His index finger lay in the bottom of a rolling paper between his thumb and middle finger. He tapped some tobacco into the paper, and returned the tobacco back to his shirt pocket. I watched as he expertly rolled the tobacco back and forth, and then licked the edge of the paper in a matter of seconds.

"Say listen; me, and my buddy was thinking of climbing to the top of that mountain today. Do you think you could keep an eye on her to see if her friends show up? I will leave my tent at the campsite for her to use tonight in case they don't." I asked.

He looked up at that mountain and then back at me, "Why in the world do you want to climb that mountain? This time of year it could snow on you, and the wind is probably blowing fifty miles per hour with gusts of seventy. It could blow you clean off the mountain!"

I smiled thinking to myself, *"Yeah, like you have ever been up there... wind blowing seventy miles an hour. Ha!"*

He watched me out of the corner of his eye as he lit the self-made cigarette. I got the eerie sense he might be reading my mind when I caught a smirk on his face. I had to wonder if just maybe he had been up there at another time in his life.

He took a long pull on the cigarette and when he stopped, the smoke that reported from it dissipated in between us. The smell of the burning tobacco brought back memories of my grandfather on the dairy in north Idaho.

"Well if you go up there, be sure to stop at that little lake nestled in those rocks, and throw a line out. It isn't a very big lake, but it is deep and there are some big ones in there!" A little wisp of smoke drifted out of his nose as he spoke.

"Thanks," I said, gazing up at the mountain of rock with the giant sliver of snow running down from the top.

He picked up his coffee cup, took one last swig and swirled the last little bit around in the cup and tossed it with the grounds into the bushes. "I am sure they will show up for her today, but I will keep an eye on her." He glanced up at the mountain towering over us and said, "Be careful. I don't want to be packing you out!"

Evelyn bid us a reluctant farewell after treating both Rob and me to pancakes, bacon, and eggs chased down with hot coffee. I told her that she could use the tent for another night if her friends did not show up, and suggested that she introduce herself to the 'ol Montana boy on the other side of the lake. She gave me a hug, and stopped short of giving Rob one when he put his backpack on. She looked so alone standing next to the tent waving good-bye as we headed for our next destination.

Rob and I picked our way carefully across the talus slope to a secluded cirque obscured in granite. As we boulder hopped over the top of a granite ridge, a small lake came into view. Sitting on the ridge above the lake was a gigantic boulder the size of a house which had fallen off the mountain. The boulder was supported by other large boulders on either side creating a small cave-like fortress. At the mouth of a cave was a level area covered in lush grass and sedges. It made a carpeted green veranda overlooking the small lake a hundred yards below. Rob and I decided to stash our backpacks and fishing poles there at the cave while we made the steep ascent up Lone Mountain.

Boulder hopping towards the summit was fun but laborious. We made good time until the mountain became vertically challenging with lose rock interspersed over the solid granite base. The loose rock made the ascent precariously unstable sending projectiles hurtling down the mountain. The higher we climbed the more strenuous it was, demanding that we use all four extremities. We methodically circled around the back side of the peak. The wind increased in intensity with the elevation gain. We were probably about five hundred yards from the top of the peak when out of nowhere a snow squall caught us off guard. We struggled to find shelter in a narrow crevice in the rock. The piercing wind blew relentlessly past the crevice howling sharply adding more severity to the perilous situation we had gotten ourselves into. Neither of us was prepared for those conditions with only a long sleeved shirt protecting us from the sudden drop in temperature. What was more alarming was the squall was starting to cover the rocks with a fine layer of snow, making any descent perilous. High on the side of that lone mountain nestled in a crevice, I whispered a small prayer. "Lord we're going to need help getting out of here!"

Rob stood up to see if he could tell how much longer the storm would last when a gust of wind hit him blowing his baseball cap off. As he reached for it the wind caught him and he lost his balance. Instinctively, I reached out and grabbed his shirt with such force that he toppled back into the crevice on top of me. His eyes expressed the fear he had just experienced. "Wow, that was close!"

The wind continued to howl as the old man's words rocked my memory. "Be careful, I don't want to pack you out of here!" The revelation hit me that what he meant was, packing us out tied over the back of a pack mule in body bags. I looked at Rob and said, "The first chance we have we need to get out of here."

As quickly as the squall hit us, it was over but the wind persisted cutting sharply through our clothes. The sun laboriously made its way through the clouds in a feeble attempt to provide a resemblance of warmth. Any residual snow able to resist the blowing wind was forced into pockets of shelter the granite provided.

Rob took a cautious step out picking his way down the mountain. Going downhill proved to be more hazardous than going uphill. Occasionally a poorly placed step sent rocks tumbling hundreds of yards down the hill across the giant field of snow before coming to rest in the boulders far below.

As I picked my way down the hill, I reached out to an outcropping of granite, and sitting alongside was a three-quarter curl bighorn sheep skull. The skull had been there so long that only one side remained intact. It was bleached white by the weather over the years, and brightly colored orange and green lichen had grown across the face. It would be a beautiful souvenir of the trip. Picking it up, I carried it in my free downhill facing hand.

We were slowly making our way just under the solid vertical peak when Rob came to a sudden stop. "Crap!" he exclaimed.

I looked beyond where Rob was standing, and my heart sank. We had worked our way around the peak and were now on the opposite side of the sliver of snow we had seen from the truck. We were near the very top of the snowdrift, and it was a good eight feet across, dropping virtually straight down while fanning out to the boulder field a thousand feet below us. We both surveyed the situation, and contemplated turning back the way we came. The sun was getting low in the sky. We would not make it back to our camp in the remaining daylight if we backtracked. Rob murmured, "I wonder how stable that snow is, or is it solid ice?"

I grabbed a large loose rock and threw it onto the head of the small glacier. It made a mark in the snow before freefalling and tumbling down the slope. We watched for what seemed like minutes before it disintegrated from view into the boulder field below. Rob turned to me and gulped before weakly saying, "Well, it's somewhat stable as long as you don't slide."

I felt like I did when I was on the high-dive at the swimming pool for the first time when I was eight years old. I wanted to throw up. "Yeah, kind of…" I replied.

There was a solid protruding finger of granite sticking up on the other side of the drift. If we happened to slide, we might be able to grab a hold of that finger of rock and it would hold us. There was no way of knowing how secure it was for sure until we got over there.

Rob looked across the eight feet of snow to the other side and then turned to me, "Rock, paper, scissors?"

I readied my hand and fist. One, two, three, and Rob's hand slapped with paper, and I came up with scissors.

Rob sighed heavily, stood up, and turned to me. "Tell my wife I love her."

Before I knew it he had launched himself halfway across the drift, placed his foot firmly in the snow, and sprung to the other side. Once there, he fumbled for stability accidentally hitting the finger of granite jutting up, knocking it lose. We both watched the rock freefall and tumble down the slope and disappear into the boulders.

Rob cleared a landing spot. Standing firmly he extended his arm towards me. "Okay buddy, I got you if you slide. Grab my arm." I looked at the footprint in the snow that Rob had left. With a big sigh, I launched myself from the safety of the solid ground, landing precisely where Rob's foot had landed, and our forearms locked at the same time. He pulled me toward him, and I landed on the solid footing Rob had cleared. I let out a deep breath, and turned back to look at the expanse of snow. That's when I noticed I had left the bighorn sheep souvenir on the other side. "Shoot!" I exclaimed.

Rob turned and asked. "Do you want to go back and get it?"

I interrupted halfway through his sentence with a firm, "No!"

The sun was low in the sky when we got back to the cave. My stomach was growling. We still had the potatoes and onion we had left with, thanks to Evelyn. Grabbing my fishing pole, I headed down towards the little lake a hundred or so yards below us. It was a unique lake, in that it was above timberline and there wasn't a solid bank around it. The edge of the lake consisted of giant precariously placed boulders. The sun was setting quickly. It would be dark soon. There wasn't a lot of time to choose the best spot to fish, so I stood on the edge of the first boulder I came to, and threw a line out. The breeze had died down to nothing in the protected basin making the water dark and still. I could not see the bottom, which gave it an even more ominous impression. The bobber had barely landed in the water when I felt a solid jerk on the end of the line. Instinctively, I raised my pole setting the hook hard. The large fish swam erratically to the right and then dodged to the left. It had hit the front fly above the streamlined bobber. I watched the bobber following wildly behind the fish when I felt another strike on the black knat off the back leader. Both fish were nice sixteen-inch cutthroat, but I had no-where to land them amongst the boulders. If I tried to lift them out of the water, their weight would break the line. Rob had just made his way down to the lake, and I asked him if he could give me a hand. Between the two of us, we were able to get them both landed, but it left my top leader all tangled up. I tried frantically to get the line untangled in the fading light to no avail. Rob landed a couple in that time with a spinner he was using. My growling stomach overrode the tangled line so I continued to fish with it tangled. We both caught a couple more before it was too dark to continue. We had plenty for dinner. I volunteered to clean the fish if Rob wanted to head up and start preparing the potatoes and onions.

When I had finished cleaning the fish and climbed back up to the cave, Rob had just finished wrapping up the potatoes and onions in aluminum foil. "We have a problem."

"Oh?" I replied. "What's that?"

"There is no wood for a fire." He retorted.

"Duh, we're above timberline huh?" I laughed.

I was so hungry I could eat everything raw.

It was dark and neither of us had a flashlight. I dug in my pocket to retrieve my lighter. Stumbling through the dark I made my way into the cave. Through the flickering light, I could make out that the floor was somewhat worn. I wondered what kind of animal had used it. I could not stand completely upright but did not have to crawl on my hands and knees either. I worked my way back about twenty feet and found what I was looking for; old "haystacks" where Pika had stored their harvests over the years. With a couple of handfuls, we could build a fast fire, enough to cook dinner on anyway. I grabbed an armful and lit a dry stalk of fireweed to provide enough light to make my way out of the back of the cave. It provided much more light than the lighter and that was when I noticed dark hair on the ceiling of the cave. A grizzly bear had used this as its winter retreat! That thought was unnerving causing me to quicken the pace back to the security of the open veranda.

Stars emerged one by one in the darkening sky as I built a roaring fire. The fragrance of the cooking potatoes and onions lingered in the air stirring hunger pangs. Gazing into the darkness, I wondered if our meal was stirring anyone else's stomach as well! There were no trees to climb if we had company in the middle of the night. We didn't have any food that needed to be tied up out of reach, but the clothes we were cooking in would have a residual odor. I mentioned what I found in the cave to Rob. After dinner, we decided to explore the cave a little further and grab another handful of dried up woody plant material for the fire.

From past experience, I knew it was probably not a good idea to explore the cave before going to sleep for the night. This was one of those times where ignorance might be bliss.

The more we explored, the more bear scat and hair we discovered in the back of the cave. We determined that it was a den previously used by a sow grizzly with cubs. Rob and I reminded each other at every opportunity that it would be quite a while before hibernation kicked in, and most likely, any bears were down in the forested areas where berries were plentiful. I thought of Evelyn screaming, and figured any bear that had been near here was now miles away anyway. We quickly exited the cave with an armload of material for the fire.

Rob built up the fire quickly announcing that he was going to sleep out under the stars on the veranda. I agreed wholeheartedly since there were no mosquitoes. As the fire died down, I spread my sleeping bag out over the gentle sedge covered veranda, and tucked myself in gazing up at the brilliant stars. The expanse of Milky Way stretched from one side of the sky to the other. The number of stars filling the sky was beyond imaginable. I drifted off to sleep as a large partial moon slowly emerged from behind the mountain; its light faded the stars back, illuminating the landscape of the wilderness below.

I flinched when the first pebble hit my cheek waking me. The second pebble hit my sleeping bag and I heard Rob whisper. "Psssst!"

"What?" I whispered back annoyed.

"Something is down there!" he said. His voice was quivering.

I listened intently, not hearing anything but my pounding heart. Suddenly, I saw movement just over the edge of the veranda. Through the moonlight, I made out a pair of pointy ears. It was a cat of some sort.

When it stepped onto the veranda next to the cold fire, I noticed how long of legs it had. I was a Lynx, not a bobcat like I had initially thought. The large cat was only about ten feet away intently searching the edge of the fire for scraps of food.

"Get outta here!" I hissed loudly waving my arms.

The Lynx jumped straight in the air, disappearing over the edge of the veranda. Occasionally the sound of a tumbling rock echoed up the hill. I had to laugh at how high the cat jumped. He wouldn't be back for a while.

When I woke up the next morning, Rob was sitting up with his back against a large rock at the entrance of the cave. He looked like he had not slept all night with his brown hair shooting out in multiple directions and his face covered with dark stubble.

I laughed and asked how he slept.

He said, "Terrible! I heard things all night long! An owl came by in the middle of the night and sat on the large rock "whooing" for about an hour.

I laughed at him.

"You never even woke up, and I ran out of pebbles to throw at you!" he continued.

"Ya, I was pretty tired," I said, crawling out of my sleeping bag.

We tried our hand at fishing before heading out and could not get a fish to even look at our bait. It was like we caught all of the fish in the lake the night before.

We packed up and headed back down the trail. No one was at the first lake where we had left Evelyn. The tent was still there but there was no note or anything. I broke down the tent quickly, and we resumed down the trail towards the trailhead. Hiking back was easy going, and we both ate berries much of the way down the hill. It was almost dark when we arrived back. The parking lot was empty as if nothing had transpired throughout the entire weekend leaving an empty feeling in my stomach. I wondered what happened to Evelyn and if the 'ol Montana man had helped her out.

This trip was so typical of how God has worked in my life over the years. Yours too, I imagine.

Our lives are full of opposition. That's just the way it is. God never said it would be easy. If anything he warned us that it would be a challenge, but not impossible. There will be days when struggles overwhelm us; everything seems hopeless, leaving us down and out, abandoned and all alone. He told us to cast our troubles upon Him. When we do, He just might send someone down the trail to help you get through it.

Conversely, when you help someone through a difficult situation you find that God will use them to bless you in a way you least expect.

God brings wise counsel into our life to help us out. It might come from His word, the Bible, or from someone along the trail. It is up to us whether we take that counsel or ignore it.

I know whenever I have ignored the wise counsel God has sent, it usually got me into a predicament where I had to get on my knees and beg God, again, to get me out of the fix I got myself into. However, through the process of the predicament God, always, showed up with a blessing in the midst of it. Every time.

We have a tendency to go through life not paying attention to how God is guiding us and the multitude of blessing He lavishes us with. It takes a conscious awareness to see God in your life. Personally, I don't believe in coincidences. When coincidences line up, it's time to take a step back and take notice of what God is doing in my life. If we are wise we learn from our previous trials to get us through other trials later in life.

I am sure you have had experiences similar to this. God tends to make these times very memorable for us so that we remember them when we get ourselves into the next predicament. And there will be another predicament. Just sayin.

Suggested Reading

Proverbs 19:17

Hebrews 13:1-3

Proverbs 12:15

Snag This:

Have you ever been in a bind and someone came along and helped you out?

Have you ever helped someone out and ended up being the one who was blessed?

Do you remember when God has sent you wise council?

Have you ever got into a bind when you did not listen to wise council?

No Fishing

"Hey, why don't you come out to the place and go fishing?" Ron asked as we walked to our rigs after work.

I was always up for fishing a new spot and Ron Allen lived on a stretch of the Gallatin River I had not been able to get on. That stretch upstream from Belgrade and north of Four Corners was strictly protected by private property so I jumped at the opportunity.

Ron and his wife, Jenny, rented a small one-bedroom farmhouse from his uncle. Ron had shared with me that he and his uncle's relationship was at times abrasive. He had vented that much of the difficulties were in regards to rent and such and he warned me to drive past the older gentleman's tan trailer quickly. He further advised me not to stop and talk to the cranky old man.

I had taken Ron's advice to heart and frantically fumbled to turn down Marshall Tucker Band blaring on the cassette when I turned onto the lane. I noticed Mr. Allen outside watering a rough looking bed of flowers as I turned in. It wasn't in my nature to be rude to my elders so I waved at him as friendly as I could. Ron had been correct in that the balding old man just glared at me in return. I sensed by the intense sneer and disdain that he had quickly placed me into the *long-haired*

101

younger generation folder. I hated being placed into that folder prematurely so did my best to drive down the lane as politely as possible in the old Ford Bronco. A previous fishing trip had knocked the muffler loose a bit which hindered some of the politeness I was trying to portray.

A barbed wire fence ran down both sides of the lane protecting an alfalfa field on one side, and a pasture of dairy cows on the other. Giant cottonwood trees grew inside the fence along the north side skirting the long lane to Ron and Jenny's tiny house. The house was quite old and looked like it needed a paint job. I noticed that the glass in one of the bedroom windows was broken and had been taped with duct tape. The 1930's era farmhouse was tucked in the midst of several large fields with an old barn and several outbuildings nearby.

They had cleaned the place up and Ron's wife, Jenny, had made the place very homey. She had even tamed a couple of the resident barn cats which dove for cover when I pulled up. The cats eventually emerged from their hiding places following us everywhere, even down to the river to go fishing. They intrigued me in that I had never seen a cat swim the river, and follow along like a dog.

When Ron and I reached the river he asked me politely which direction I wanted to fish. I pointed up the river and he said, "Okay, I will meet you back at the place at dark." I watched in amazement as the cats followed Ron across the river downstream.

Wading my way upstream I fished the holes and pockets with a Black Panther Martin with a gold flasher and yellow spots on the body. This same lure had great success on the East Gallatin River the previous week.

The fish were hitting the black and gold lure here too. Almost every cast I got a strike. I noticed a back eddy up ahead that swirled alongside a partially obscured log tucked into the bank. I cast up to the edge of where the root wad protruded over the river letting the small lure sink into the head of the eddy. As I began to retrieve it, the lure stopped bending the end of the fishing pole firmly. At first, I thought I was hung up on the bottom but as I held constant pressure on the snag I felt the head shake and the large fish gave ground. I steadily reeled lifting the large fish from his underwater lair. He shook his head savagely as he neared the surface and then rolled just under the surface barely making a splash. I watched in disbelief as the dark spots embossed with light halos against the massive brownish yellow side came into view. Frantically I fumbled to adjust the drag, when with a flick of its giant tail the large fish snapped the line and disappeared. My heart immediately sank. Disappointed weakness worked through the muscles in my arms and legs which deposited a tingling sensation at each joint. My legs quivered in adrenaline induced disbelief as I watched my slack line coiled at my feet float unrestrained downstream. Solemnly, I retreated back to shore to retie a new swivel on my line replaying the scenario over and over in my mind. *"That was a huge fish."* My hands were shaking as I tried put on another lure. It was beginning to get dark. I cast several more times into the eddy in faded hope the large fish would hit again.

I barely noticed the herd of cows following me through the field on the way back to the house. The giant fish was consuming my thoughts and I jumped when the black and white cat appeared suddenly in the dark.

"Yeah, there are some hogs in that river!" Ron exclaimed when I told him the story of the big fish. " I caught a couple of nice ones tonight too but let them all go except for this guy, "Ron stated, displaying a large five-pound rainbow. "I prefer to eat the smaller ones because the big ones taste terrible!"

The rainbow was still much larger than a majority of the fish I had caught with the exception of the bruiser.

Ron eyed the Panther Martin dangling off the end of my fishing pole.

"Did you catch the big one on that lure?" he asked.

I nodded.

He said, "You typically can't catch those big 'ol boys on a lure like that." My uncle used to out-fish me every time when I first moved here. Then I watched what he fished with. He used a sculpin for bait, drifting it through the holes. When I watched how he fished I began using sculpin too, and graduated from the little guys to the hogs!" Ron explained.

The rest of the week visions of the large brown permeated my mind during work. I couldn't wait to get out and try again with this new technique.

One day, Ron didn't show up to work. It was the middle of September. Steve, our supervisor at the brickyard said that Ron had called in and resigned after work the previous day. He said that Ron had told him that he was moving to Colorado and was leaving early the next day. I knew Ron's wife Jenny had a sister in Colorado, and assumed they were moving to be closer to family. After all, they didn't seem to get along well with his estranged uncle.

Still, this abrupt news was a shock. I spent most of the day in a slump. I was going to miss Ron, and his crazy sense of humor. But there was something else, how was I ever going to fish that stretch of the river again? That monster trout haunted me day and night. I thought of asking his uncle, Mr. Allen, if I could cross the property to go fishing, but the remembrance of his ornery sneer caused me to hesitate. I had to somehow reflect a portrait of upstanding character to counteract his preconceived judgment on me.

School started at Montana State University and one of my roommates threw a small get together with some of his classmates. I happened to come into the party late that Friday night, and was reporting to my roommate about fishing on the East Fork of the Gallatin River on the way home. There was a large culvert under the highway where I would occasionally stop, and throw a lure up into. I told my roommate, Red, about a nice sized rainbow I caught that afternoon. I noticed a fellow student from across the room listening intently when I mentioned the lunker. His eyes looked away, but he could not hide the fact that he was hanging on every word I said. When he sidestepped in our direction between two girls who were talking, it made me laugh out loud. Red asked where I was fishing, and Dan could not contain himself any longer. "I had a huge one on at that same culvert last week!" He said excitedly. "Did you land him?"

I said "No! He got off!"

Dan Danielson and I became the best of friends from that moment on. He and fishing proved to be detrimental to my first year of higher education. I made the Dean's List, but not in a way to write home about.

One day I relayed the story of the large brown that had gotten away on the West Gallatin River to Dan, and the perplexing problem of getting on that property to fish. Now Dan was an eternal optimist, and he convinced me that we should go down and have a "good 'ol boy" conversation with Mr. Allen.

"After all, we are good 'ol boys too!" He said.

The next day, with all of Dan's optimism, we went to visit Mr. Allen. He answered the door, and I could tell he recognized me by the snarl on his face. I did my best to maintain Dan's optimism saying, "Howdy!" which had no effect on his demeanor.

"What do you want?" the old man demanded.

"Well," I stuttered, my optimism was fading quickly, "We were just wondering if we could cross your property to do a little fishing on the river?"

"Have you been fishing down there?" he replied sharply.

"Oh, this was good!" I thought. With a little communication, I could show him some of my upstanding character. Mentioning Ron might buy me a little grace on this so I decided to do a little name-dropping. "Uh, yes sir, just once, when Ron and Jenny lived down in the little house."

"Ron? That worthless nephew of mine? He left in the middle of the night, and stuck me with a month and a half rent." He said angrily "No, Not today!" He said through the screen door.

"Oh, I didn't know him very well... I just knew him from w... !" I desperately explained. The words were lost in the slamming door.

Dan and I climbed back into the Bronco. "Well," Dan said, "he didn't say no! We will try it again when he is in a better mood!"

As spring emerged from winter the memory of that big brown came back alive. One day on the way home from school, I decided to stop by and visit with Mr. Allen. He recognized me as soon as he opened the door. I never gave him a chance to say a word. "Sir, I don't mean to bother you, but I would sure like to go fishing on the river. Could I please get permission to cross your place?"

I caught the balding old man actually crack a smile when he said, "No, I don't want anybody back there right now, I just planted that back field."

I nodded understanding, but left feeling like I was gaining headway. He at least cracked a smile. I was optimistic that eventually, he would let me go fishing. In the meantime, I thought of every possible angle to swing things my way.

One day, my girlfriend, Anna and I were passing by Mr. Allen's place. I let out a big sigh as we passed. She asked me what that was all about, and I explained to her about Mr. Allen and the whole fishing dilemma.

She listened patiently, and suggested that maybe cookies would work?

"Cookies?" I replied.

"Yeah, maybe the 'ol boy has a sweet tooth?' she said. "My grandmother always said, *You can catch more flies with honey, than you can with vinegar!*"

I envisioned handing Mr. Allen a plate of homemade cookies, and having him break into a big 'ol smile, embracing me with one arm before waving me on down the lane to fish that coveted stretch of river.

"Anna, you gotta help me cook up some cookies!" I said excitedly. I couldn't wait to try out this sure-fire plan.

The following Friday, I stopped by where Anna worked. She had a dozen cookies double paper-plated, and covered with aluminum foil. The smell of them in the warm car was intoxicating. This was the secret. Unfortunately, Anna had to work all weekend so she bid me farewell on my endeavor.

I confidently approached Mr. Allen's door proudly displaying the plate of cookies in my hand. Surely this would work, I thought. When he answered the door I could see the surprise as he eyed the plate of cookies.

He then cautiously eyed me, and slowly opened the screen door. "What'cha got there?" he asked.

I pulled up a corner of the aluminum foil exposing the freshly baked cookies.

"I figured maybe I could bribe you into letting me go fishing with these homemade chocolate chip cookies!"

"Hmmmm.... " he said cautiously "Did you bake these?"

"No" I laughed," my girlfriend did."

Mr. Allen grabbed one of the cookies and tasted it. His eyes closed showing how good the cookie was. It was almost embarrassing how much he enjoyed the bite in complete bliss. When he could speak he asked, "Is your girlfriend here? "

"No, she is working," I replied smiling.

"Tell her, *Thank you*," he said grabbing another cookie, and pulling the aluminum foil back over the rest of them. "They are really good!"

I stood there dumbfounded holding the plate of cookies as he started to close the door.

"Well... can I go fishing?" I clamored in complete surprise.

"Oh, no, I rented out the place down the lane, and I can't imagine they would appreciate having someone walk through their yard." And with that, he shut the door.

I left dejected realizing that I would probably never get into that fishing hole again.

Still that large brown haunts me, but I have given up on the dream of fishing that stretch of river. I have come to the point where I am satisfied with the memory of the time I did get to fish that part of the Gallatin, and that giant brown trout gets bigger every year!

Have you ever done that with God? You pray for something, and He doesn't answer right away? First, you get yourself all honorable and righteous before coming to His throne, asking Him in the confidence of your self-righteousness with a carefully worded prayer.

When you get no answer, you go to Him again pleading with all of your heart.

Then you come right out and reason with Him, thinking that maybe if you are totally honest with Him, He will answer your prayer.

Sometimes we want our prayer answered so badly we go as far as to manipulate or even try to bribe Him.

Each time He answers the door with a "Not now" or a "Maybe later" leaving us standing frustrated on the step. Eventually, we come to the realization that it is not meant to be, and we might as well stop knocking on that door. Through the whole process of prayer, He is working on us to accept the "No." As time passes we might eventually understand why he gave us the "No" and ultimately be thankful that answer.

I am still waiting to understand the reason for that particular "No", but I am confident the Lord will explain when I get to heaven.

Suggested Reading

James 4:3-10

2 Corinthians 12:8-10

Snag This:

Have you ever asked God for something and got a definite "No"?

Did you try to persuade Him or manipulate Him to get an answer?

Do you think you were asking in accordance to His will?

Have you ever been thankful for unanswered prayers?

Proactive Fishing

A thin ribbon of ice curled up with each revolution from the ice auger. My arm was getting sore, and I was only ten inches into a two-foot layer of ice. Mark was rigging up his pole, and Larry was twenty feet away with his line in the water jigging.

Mark and Larry were brothers. Larry's wife worked with Julie, my wife at the Forest Service. I met Larry at a Forest Service Christmas party, and we naturally got talking about hunting and fishing. Julie and I had recently moved to central Idaho and didn't know many people yet. Larry invited me to go fishing on Cascade Lake for the notorious monster Perch. I jumped at the opportunity to learn more about my new home and what better way to learn than from someone who had been born and raised in the small central Idaho town we lived in. Larry was eager to welcome me along, but Mark wasn't especially fond of sharing one of his favorite fishing spots. I knew I was going to have to prove myself to Mark, and that drove me to work even harder to auger the hole in the ice.

Fresh lake water gushed out of the hole as I lifted the auger out. Having the hole drilled through the thick ice, I was relieved to give my arms a break by removing the residual slush with the ladle. The night before, I had made five of my homemade tip-ups. It was a simple design with material lying around in the garage. They each consisted of a 1"x2"x12" piece of pine with a notch cut in each end. I bent a coat hanger into the shape of a "V" and nailed the valley of the V with a horseshoe nail to the center of the board. Then I secured the fishing line to the board and wrapped about 60 feet of twenty pound fishing line end to end, length-wise on the board. On one side of the coat hanger, I tied flagging that I had in my hunting pack. On the other side, I bent the coat hanger into an open loop to hold the line that went on down to the baited hook in the ice hole.

I lowered the line down to the bottom before raising it up about ten feet, and set it down next to the freshly augured hole when Mark said, "They're not here. Let's move!"

Larry responded immediately by reeling up his line quickly. I was shocked and somewhat annoyed since I just barely got my line wet after sweating through the chore of auguring through two feet of solid ice. Mark had his line reeled up, and the snowmobile started while I was still wrapping up my line on the tip-up. Larry was sitting on his snow machine impatiently waiting for me to get it together as Mark headed off. I didn't have a snow machine so Larry was waiting on me. I scrambled to load up my pack and tip-ups on the sled, and get on the back of the snow machine.

Mark, was already two hundred yards away, and in the process of drilling a new hole in the ice. By the time we got there, he was clearing his hole with the ladle. Larry grabbed the auger and started drilling a hole, twenty feet away. I grabbed my pack and set up twenty feet from both of them. While I waited for the auger, I got my tip-up ready to be dropped into the hole. I watched Mark as he fished. He stood at the hole with a small fishing pole jigging several times then let it sit for about thirty seconds. As I grabbed the auger, Mark had a fish on. I figured that meant we would stay put for a while. By the time I had my hole drilled, Larry caught one and Mark had caught another smaller one. I quickly dropped my line into the water and set my tip-up at the edge of the hole and stood back to wait for a bite. Mark was eying the ice surrounding us. "Keep an eye on my pole."

He grabbed the auger and walked past me sixty yards toward shore and started drilling. After he had drilled the hole he walked back to where we were. As he passed me to get his fishing pole he stated, "Check your line, you're probably out of bait." I picked up my tip-up and pulled the lineup. Sure enough, my bait was gone.

"How did you know that?" I asked.

Larry laughed at me. "They are biting light. Run the line through your fingers."

"No way, not that light! Are they?" I argued.

"That's why we use these small rods, so we can tell when they are biting."

I was just dropping my line down after re-baiting the hook when Larry said. "We better move over by Mark before he catches them all."

I looked over where Mark was pulling up a nice fat perch and another one was flopping on the ice. Larry and I moved the snow machines over and re-drilled holes around Mark and settled in on fishing. Within an hour, we came home with a five-gallon bucket apiece of fourteen-inch perch.

Spring runoff brought with it the annual Chinook salmon season on the Little Salmon River. I had driven past it on highway 95. It was an impressive site. Fisherman were lined-up shoulder to shoulder through a one mile stretch of tumultuous rapids. The giant fish had to pass through this gauntlet of fisherman, and another stretch of the river set aside for Native Americans with nets and spears before entering the hatchery up Rapid River. I had never fished that season because it was what I considered *combat fishing* which never appealed to me.

I happened to run into Larry at the post office while checking the mail. It was still too wet to do any logging in the high country so he and Mark had been fishing for salmon. "We're going tomorrow if you want to go."

I was working in fisheries and wildlife for the Krassel Ranger District and didn't work the next day, but the thought of fighting all of those people did not appeal to me in the least. I laughed and said, "No Thanks! That sounds miserable."

Larry said, "Okay, just so you know, we know people that have private land just below the rapids."

"When did you say I should be at your house?" I asked excitedly.

The next morning Larry, Mark and I drove north towards Riggins. We had to slow down to a crawl as we drove along that stretch of highway. There were rigs parked on both sides of the road. Fishermen casually walked across the highway with their fishing gear in hand like they were walking across a parking lot. The Little Salmon River had been mobbed by fishermen of every shape and size.

Larry pulled into a heavily posted, vacant lot, just below the public access. There were a handful of people fishing along the bank, but nothing like the elbow to elbow fisherman on the public access. The spring runoff had the river boiling at the top of its banks. I was unsure how anyone could even get a fish to bite in such a raging torrent. All a twenty-pound fish needed to do was turn side-ways, and it would be swept down the stream. I was contemplating this while watching Mark fish. He had walked directly up between two guys, and cast at the edge of the river. Both fishermen glanced at Mark, and his intrusion on their portion of the bank.

Each of them reluctantly took a step to the side. Mark never bothered to acknowledge either of them. On his third cast, Mark forcefully set the hook.

"Fish On!" he hollered, looking back towards me. I knew he wanted the net. His pole almost bent in half as he horsed the fish quickly to the bank against the fast-moving river. I hustled to the river's edge scrambling along the shore. Mark reeled down close to the large fish, and with a steady pull, rolled the salmon towards shore. I plunged the net downstream of the large fish just as Mark let up on the tension. The twenty-five-pound fish rolled, in a last attempt to get away, right into the net. I quickly hauled it up onto the bank to inspect the fish. The adipose fin had been clipped marking it as a keeper. I handed the net to Mark, and stepped into his spot with my fishing pole. I fished in the same spot for about an hour with no luck when Larry walked by with a salmon he had caught downstream.

"Have any luck"? He asked, grinning from ear to ear.

I shook my head, eying the salmon jealously as he walked by. Larry walked close and whispered, "Fish along shore. That's where they're lying."

Larry asked if I knew where Mark was, and I nodded upstream. Mark was wedging himself in between two other fishermen on the public ground. They both gave him a dirty look as Mark cast upstream close to shore.

Almost immediately, his pole shot down and went up as he set the hook. His pole bobbing frantically. I shook my head in disbelief. *"How in the world do these guys do this?"* I wondered. The guys on either side forgetting about Mark's aggressiveness reeled in quickly to assist him to land the large fish. Mark obviously knew what he was doing, and that demanded respect for his direct approach. Within an hour both Mark and Larry had limited out, and I had one on the bank after following their instructions. On the way home I thought about their approach to Salmon fishing. I had to admire Mark and Larry for their zealous no-nonsense determination.

I didn't see much of the Callahan brothers all that summer. I was in the backcountry working, and they were busy cutting timber.

Towards the end of fall later that year I ran into Larry down at Brown's Market in town. He was showing several local guys a nice whitetail buck that his daughter had shot. The guys were all standing around the bed of the truck drooling at the big buck. I swung in to check it out too. After much congratulating, and exchanging hunting stories, we set out on our separate ways. As I was climbing into my truck Larry shouted from his truck "Hey! I hear the steelhead are in the Big River. *(referring to the main Salmon River)* Let's go fishing Friday."

I nodded in approval with a *"thumbs up"* through the passenger window and headed home.

Mark and Larry picked me up at my place early Friday morning, and we headed north towards Riggins. I had caught a few steelhead on the Clearwater River up north but had never fished the main Salmon River for steelhead so I looked forward to furthering my education. I had learned to keep an eye on these two guys when it came to hunting or fishing.

When Mark stopped the truck along the highway, I was wondering why he stopped in that particular spot. There was barely enough room to pull off the highway, and the bank down to the river was steep with only a vague trail. I hung back a little to observe as both Mark and Larry bee-lined it to the shore. Larry beat Mark and cast out a light orange corkie with a shrimp into the middle of the river. Mark cast upstream from Larry's line bumping along the bottom. Just as I cast upstream from Mark's line, Larry jerked his pole back setting the hook and his line went taut. "Fish On!" he laughed.

I reeled in quickly while Larry played the eight-pound sea-going trout. Mark seeing that I was going to net the fish, continued fishing. I had just netted Larry's steelhead when Mark hooked a large female. I remained on net duty while Larry untangled his line, re-baited his hook and went back to fishing. After netting the fish I handed the net with the fish still in it to Mark and I joined Larry fishing the obscure hole. Mark cleaned both of the fish and when he was finished he said "Ready?"

Larry responded immediately "Yup" and started reeling in his line.

"Are we done?" I said in surprise.

"We are here anyway!" Mark said heading back to where the truck was parked.

I reeled in quickly and caught up to Larry. He looked at me smiling knowing that I was curious why we were leaving so soon. "This time of year there are usually only a couple of fish per hole." He explained, "We don't like to spend a lot of time waiting for new fish to come into the hole so we just move on to the next hole."

I thought about that as we drove to the next hole. I was riding shotgun so when the truck stopped I wasted no time getting out. I grabbed my rod, and bee-lined-it towards the hole. I reached the fishing hole first, and cast my pale green corkie to the head of the hole. I kept my line taut reeling steadily watching my tip as the lead weight bounced down through the deep hole. Suddenly it stopped and I pulled. My line erupted in wild frenzy as the brightly colored steelhead shot to the head of the hole before launching in the air swatting the rivers surface, determined to shake the hook loose. He made several runs throughout the hole causing my drag to sing. Finally, he tired enough for Mark to net the wild fish. He was a lunker, a whopping thirty-eight inches weighing close to 16 pounds, but there was no denying that adipose fin right before the tail. It was a wild steelhead and needed to be released. Since I didn't have a camera with me, I measured him with a willow I had cut from along shore. Now I have that impressive willow hanging on the wall in the office.

I learned a lot about fishing and application in regards to our Christian walk from the Callahan brothers. Many of us tend to be passive fishermen. We go fishing throwing our line out, and let the line sit there dangling in hopes that a fish comes along and takes the bait. As the Callahan's proved to me consistently with fishing as well as pheasant, chukar and elk hunting, there is more success in being proactive. They never settled on chance, they made things happen.

It the same with our Christian walk. A majority of Christians have a tendency to relax, and become complacent after they have been a Christian for a while. They hole up together and don't intermingle with non-Christians. Surrounded by other Christians is a safe zone where there is little persecution. They will share their faith if someone sits next to them in church but are not proactive about it. Fellowship is important, but Jesus called us to go out into the world and make disciples for Christ. Just because we got saved doesn't mean the game ended. The game just began! Why not get out where fishing is more lucrative. The bank might be steeper and the trail is less traveled but the fishing is much better. How many fish do you have on your stringer? The nice part about this kind of fishing is there are no limit or size restrictions.

What I learned from the Calahan brothers is to pay attention to any opportunity to share the Good News of Jesus. If one approach doesn't work then hit it from a different angle till you find one that works. Sometimes you need to bust through the crowd and get in the midst of them. They might not like you initially, but when you share with them what you know, they will be forever grateful.

Suggested Reading

Matthew 28:16-20

Acts 1:7-8

Snag This:

Are you a patient fisherman or proactive fisherman?

What ministry you would like to be involved with?

What talents has the Lord given you to reach out to more people?

The Cycle is Complete

"Dad, you have to go fishing down there with me!" I exclaimed, holding up the large four-pound smallmouth bass.

"Where did you catch that?" Dad asked, eyeing me in my ironed shirt, dress slacks, and dress shoes.

"Downtown, along the dike," I said excitedly. "After my meeting with Shelley, I was driving across the bridge, and I heard the bass calling! I had to stop and throw a line out."

Dad laughed at my excitement, shaking his head as I continued. "I was catching them right and left," I said "I have got it dialed in baby! You just have to barely reel dragging the plastic jig ever so slowly over the rocks" I said slowly, pretending to reel with my air fishing rod "and... WHAM!! Fish On!"

"Dad, you gotta go," I pleaded "It's a level walking path down the dike. I can help you down to the river. There's a level pebble beach and a log you can sit on."

Dad had recently turned seventy-two, and after a failed eye surgery in one eye his depth perception was off. He was very leery about going anyplace off the pavement. His confidence had been shaken recently, especially after he had taken a spill in the lobby at the bank. He had joked about it with mom and I, but I could tell it bothered him quite a bit. He had come to the conclusion that he was getting old, and this was going to be the way it was from here on out.

I wasn't ready for him to give up just yet. For the last few weeks, I had dropped off some of the bass I had caught in hopes it might persuade him to go fishing with me. This time I wasn't going to take "No" for an answer.

I could see dad contemplating as he looked at me and then the large bass. I didn't give him a chance to turn me down saying, "I am going home to change clothes, and will be back in an hour to pick you up."

I stuck pretty close to him as he walked on wobbly legs over the parkway bridge and down the paved walking path. He wore his fishing vest and I had to laugh when I saw the old dilapidated straw hat tucked in the large game pocket in back. His walk was unsteady even on the pavement and he leaned heavily on my arm as we got off the pavement working our way down to the little pebble beach. I kicked a few of the larger rocks out of the way, hoping it was actually level enough for him. I tied on a fresh, black jig with a chartreuse tail while explaining to him how to reel slowly across the bottom and how to stop and twitch the line just a hair to make the big bass bite. I stood next to him as he made his first cast, and he got hung up on the bottom. He was having a hard time getting it un-snagged so I gave him a hand. I was not able to get the lure un-snagged and ended up having to break the line. While I was tying a new lure on I encouraged him.

"I always lose some tackle getting hung up on the bottom. If you're going to get the big ones, you have to get your jig where they hang out."

Dad commented on all of the small minnows rising to the surface at the edge of the current. I explained to him that they were Chinook Salmon fry being flushed downstream by the high spring run-off on their way to the ocean. These were what the bass were gorging on and why the big ones hung out right along shore at this time.

On his next cast, he reeled in a little quicker keeping it off the bottom but never got a bite. I fished next to him for a while and caught several small bass. He seemed to be doing pretty good, and wasn't having any problems standing on shore. I sensed that it was frustrating him seeing me catch fish, when he wasn't even getting a bite. I sensed that he needed a little space, so I grabbed a handful of leaded jig heads, and set them on the large log with a variety of plastic jigs.

"Here are some extra jig heads, I am going to give it a try over by those large rocks."

I found a large boulder to fish off of and got, caught up deep in thought about how dad had suddenly gotten old. I hoped that he would catch a nice bass. As I was envisioning this in my mind, I heard a loud commotion back where dad was. When I turned to look, I was shocked to see dad had fallen backward over the log. He was lying on his back with his pole lifted high, feet up in the air still draped over the log with his cowboy boots kicking frantically in the air. He turned and looked over at me with a big smile on his face. "I got one!" His pole was doubled over, the tip dancing wildly. A two-pound bass thrashed the water before diving in a frantic attempt to remove the jig that had securely hooked his jaw.

I reeled my line in quickly and went over to help dad. He handed me the pole. I was doing my best not to laugh at him as I helped him back up over the log. He was a big guy, and it wasn't easy. I secured the pole on the ground, and used both hands to get him back up over the log. We both got to laughing so hard that we didn't notice the bass was pulling the pole into the water. Dad spotted it and I leaped to retrieve it before it disappeared in the river. Through the process, the reel got all tangled up in a complete rat's nest. I pulled the bass in by hand and put it on the stringer. Dad was having a difficult time untangling the mess so I went to where he was sitting on the log. "Here give it to me," I said.

He gladly handed it to me. It was a mess. I sat next to him on the log, sighed heavily and said, "Man, how did this happen?"

Dad, with a smile on his face and a twinkle in his eye, said. "Well, the cycle is now complete."

I laughed and thought about the depth of that statement not really wanting to admit how true it was. The line was so tangled, it was easier to cut it off and put a new swivel on it. Dad and I sat on the log reminiscing about all of the times when he had untangled me and my sister's lines. Listening to him laugh about it I could see that there was a blessing in it for him. The patience he had endured over the years had perfected into a blessing.

Conversely watching his patience with us kids, has helped us be patient in life when we had a mess to deal with. We learned early on how to untangle problems a little at a time.

That got me to thinking about how God shows us the same patience and through His lead, we learn to work through struggles in our lives and that in turn, glorifies Him. In the Bible, in the book of James, it states in Chapter 2:1 *"My brethren, count it all joy when you fall into various trials, knowing that the testing of your faith produces patience. But let patience have its perfect work, that you may be perfect and complete, lacking nothing."*

This was part of the final package for Dad, *"perfect and complete, lacking nothing"* from a fisherman's perspective. I was honored to sit there on the log and experience that blessing with him. With dad's fish, we had enough for dinner so we called it a day.

That was Dad's last cast.

A month later Dad lost his balance going up the stairs. He fell backward hitting his head on the cement floor, and died instantly.

It just goes to show how fleeting this life can be. We never know when our last day will be. God, through His love and grace, has given us all a lifetime of free choices to have a relationship with Him. When you look back on your life, you will see definitive times when God undoubtedly has been there doing His best to get your attention. Reading this book might just be another one of those nudges. What you do with His invitation is entirely up to you, but keep in mind, it has eternal consequences. The Bible says that there is only one way to the Father, and that is through His Son, Jesus Christ. God has done everything for you to make that decision as easy as possible, but He loves you so much that He has given you the choice to make it for yourself.

Heaven or Hell? For all of eternity.

One or the other, there is no other option.

God sent Jesus, His only Son, as a sacrifice for each of our sins. All we have to do is acknowledge, yes, I am sinner, believe that Jesus died for my sins and ask Jesus to come into my heart. Jesus will send the Holy Spirit into our life and He will transform our life. The Bible states in Revelation 3:20 *"Behold, I stand at the door and knock; if any man hear my voice, and open the door, I will come in to him, and sup with him, and he with Me."*

Pretty simple, huh? No big dramatic prayer is needed. Just be honest and real.

When I asked Jesus into my heart all I said was, "Jesus, I need help." That was July 28, 1996, at 4:28 in the morning. My life was transformed in the most amazing way, and I never looked back! It was the best decision I ever made, and there has never been a dull moment since!

The last words Jesus spoke as He was hanging on the cross was, *Tetelestai,* in Greek or, "It is Finished." That is kind of like what Dad said in a roundabout way...

The cycle is now complete.

Suggested Reading

Revelation 20:11-15

Snag This:

Have you seen where God has tried to get your attention?

Where are you at with your personal relationship with Jesus?

Like all relationships, have you been investing time into your relationship with Jesus?

Acknowledgments

First and foremost, all glory goes to God the Father.
Without His prompting, this book would not have been
written. I feel blessed to have had the pleasure to fish
with so many men and women over the years.

Lloyd M. Cox – My dad. I am so thankful for him. He
taught me how to laugh, and not to take life too
seriously. He also introduced me to hunting and fishing.
I think I had the best childhood any kid could have. He
was my best friend, and I miss him dearly.

Sarah Jones – Sarah is like a daughter to me. I am so
thankful for her editing wisdom, sense of humor, and
encouragement.

Brenda Mahler – Brenda is so gifted with her editing
wisdom and has blessed me so much with her talent.

Laurie Koga – Laurie has been my side-kick a majority of
my life. She has done her best to keep me out of trouble
and that has been a full-time job. I appreciate her
honesty, accountability and value her sense of humor
and friendship.

Jenny Jones – Jenny is the epitome of encouragement. I
so appreciate her love for the Lord and her love for
everyone she meets to have a loving relationship with

Jesus. She is a true evangelist and what a good friend she is!

Lori Nicolls – I appreciate Lori's sense of humor and wisdom. She is a good proofreader and someone who I value bouncing ideas off of. So many nights Nick, Lori and I discuss writing and get to laughing so hard we cannot stand up. That's the good stuff!

Nick Nicolls – My friend Nick... doesn't that sound like a good book? I have so many stories I could tell, but, so does he. He is the brother I never had. Nick has put up with all of my creative idiosyncrasies over the years. I appreciate his ear and patience while I relentlessly work out the stories in the books.

If this book has touched your heart and changed your direction in life I would love to hear from you. You can contact me through the address at the front of the book.

Thanks and God Bless YOU!
Bill

If you enjoyed this book, check out these other books written by William H. Cox at:
www.rustyironranchllc.com

The unconditional love of
A Dog's Love

ISBN-13: 978-0692716366 (Rusty Iron Ranch, LLC)
ISBN-10: 069271636X

Skies Are Not Cloudy All Day
Is God trying to get your attention?

ISBN-13: 978-1-312-93832-8 (Rusty Iron Ranch, LLC)

32716934R00078

Made in the USA
Columbia, SC
13 November 2018